FORAGING IDAHO

FORAGING IDAHO

Finding, Identifying, and Preparing
Edible Wild Foods

Christopher Nyerges

GUILFORD, CONNECTICUT

An imprint of The Rowman & Littlefield Publishing Group, Inc.
4501 Forbes Blvd., Ste. 200
Lanham, MD 20706
www.rowman.com

Falcon and FalconGuides are registered trademarks and Make Adventure Your Story is a trademark of
The Rowman & Littlefield Publishing Group, Inc.

Distributed by NATIONAL BOOK NETWORK

British Library Cataloguing-in-Publication Information available

Library of Congress Cataloging in Publication Data:

Names: Nyerges, Christopher, author.
Title: Foraging Idaho : finding, identifying, and preparing edible wild foods / Christopher Nyerges.
Description: Guilford, Connecticut ; Helena, Montana : FalconGuides, [2018] |
   Includes bibliographical references and index.
Identifiers: LCCN 2018003166 (print) | LCCN 2018007156 (ebook) | ISBN 9781493031917 (ebook) |
   ISBN 9781493031900 (pbk.)
Subjects: LCSH: Wild plants, Edible--Idaho. | Wild plants, Edible—Idaho—Identification.
Classification: LCC QK98.5.U6 (ebook) | LCC QK98.5.U6 N9385 2018 (print) |
   DDC 581.6/3209796—dc23
LC record available at https://lccn.loc.gov/2018003166

∞™ The paper used in this publication meets the minimum requirements of American National Standard
for Information Sciences—Permanence of Paper for Printed Library Materials, ANSI/NISO Z39.48-1992.

Printed in the United States of America

The identification, selection, and processing of any wild plant for use as food requires reasonable care and attention to details since, as indicated in the text, certain parts are wholly unsuitable for use and, in some instances, are even toxic. Because attempts to use any wild plants for food depend on various factors controllable only by the reader, the author and Globe Pequot assume no liability for personal accident, illness, or death related to these activities.

This book is a work of reference. Readers should always consult an expert before using any foraged item. The author, editors, and publisher of this work have checked with sources believed to be reliable in their efforts to confirm the accuracy and completeness of the information presented herein and that the information is in accordance with the standard practices accepted at the time of publication. However, neither the author, editors, and publisher, nor any other party involved in the creation and publication of this work, warrant that the information is in every respect accurate and complete, and they are not responsible for errors or omissions or for any consequences from the application of the information in this book. In light of ongoing research and changes in clinical experience and in governmental regulations, readers are encouraged to confirm the information contained herein with additional sources. This book does not purport to be a complete presentation of all plants, and the genera, species, and cultivars discussed or pictured herein are but a small fraction of the plants found in the wild, in an urban or suburban landscape, or in a home. Given the global movement of plants, we would expect continual introduction of species having toxic properties to the regions discussed in this book. We have made every attempt to be botanically accurate, but regional variations in plant names, growing conditions, and availability may affect the accuracy of the information provided. A positive identification of an individual plant is most likely when a freshly collected part of the plant containing leaves and flowers or fruits is presented to a knowledgeable botanist or horticulturist. Poison Control Centers generally have relationships with the botanical community should the need for plant identification arise. We have attempted to provide accurate descriptions of plants, but there is no substitute for direct interaction with a trained botanist or horticulturist for plant identification. **In cases of exposure or ingestion, contact a Poison Control Center (1-800-222-1222), a medical toxicologist, another appropriate heathcare provider, or an appropriate reference resource.**

CONTENTS

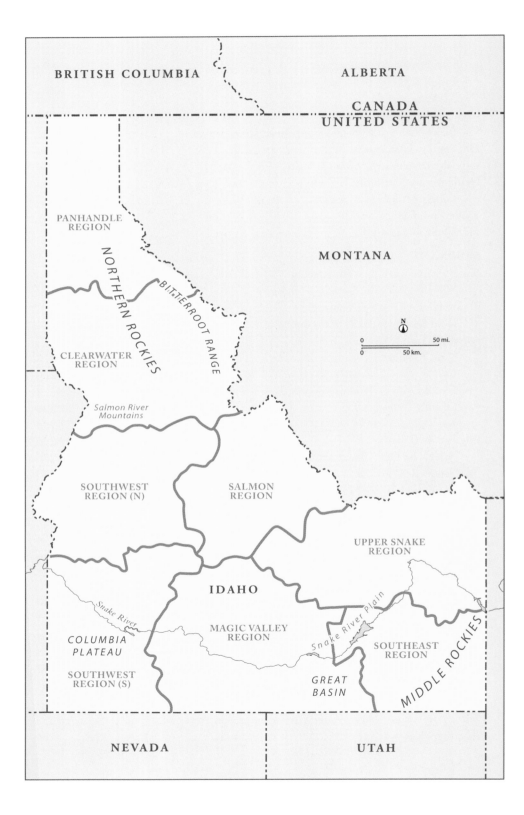

ACKNOWLEDGMENTS

My primary ethnobotanical mentor was Dr. Leonid Enari, whom I first met in 1975. Dr. Enari's unique background in botany and chemistry made him ideally suited as a primary source of information. He earned higher degrees in both botany and chemistry (equivalent to PhDs) in his twenties before emigrating to the United States from Estonia, where he had experienced some of the results of Nazi occupation. He would tell his students that he pursued these fields because he desired to help people. "With the knowledge of botany and chemistry," he once told our class, "no one need ever go hungry."

When he first moved to the United States, he settled in Portland, Oregon, and taught at Lewis and Clark College and the University of Portland. While living in the Northwest, Dr. Enari researched and wrote *Plants of the Pacific Northwest*, the result of about forty field trips. I have used that book as one of my primary references. He eventually moved to Southern California.

Dr. Enari acted as my teacher, mentor, and friend, and he always encouraged me on to further research as well as teaching and writing. He assisted me with my first book, *Guide to Wild Foods* , and also consulted on my various botanical writing projects.

I felt the great loss when he passed away in 2006 at age eighty-nine.

To Dr. Enari, I dedicate this book on Idaho's wild foods.

I also had many other mentors, teachers, and supporters along the way. These include (but are not limited to) Dr. Luis Wheeler (botanist), Richard Barmakian (nutritionist), Dorothy Poole (Gabrielino "chaparral granny"), Richard E. White (founder of WTI, who taught me how to teach, and how to think; it was through WTI that I began teaching); John Watkins (a Mensan who "knew everything"), and Mr. Muir (my botany teacher at John Muir High School). These individuals all imparted some important aspect to me, and they have all been my mentors to varying degrees. I thank them for their influence. Euell Gibbons also had a strong influence on my early studies of wild food, mostly through his books; I met him only once.

Nearly twenty years ago I met John Kallas, who I regard as the top wild-food man of the Pacific Northwest. Kallas's field trips, workshops, and books are strongly recommended for anyone living in Idaho, the Northwest, and the surrounding area. With a doctorate in botany, he is a remarkable resource for the Northwest.

Of course, there have been many others who taught me bits and pieces along the way, and I feel gratitude for everyone whose love of the multifaceted art of ethnobotany has touched me in some way. Some of these friends, associates, and strong supporters have included Pascal Baudar and Mia Wasilevich, Peter Gail,

Gary Gonzales, Dude McLean, Alan Halcon, Paul Campbell, Rick and Karen Adams, Barbara Kolander, Jim Robertson, Timothy Snider, and Dr. Norman Wakeman.

I want to extend a special thanks to my beloved wife, Helen, for her support of this time-consuming project!

I also wish to give special thanks to William Schlegel and Kyle Chamberlain, who assisted with many of the details of this manuscript. In addition, I thank the other botanists who assisted with this project, who chose to remain unnamed.

Photo Credits

Yes, I took many of the photos in this book, but I couldn't do it all myself. Rick Adams deserves special thanks for the many trips we took together to get photos. Other folks who contributed photos include my dear Helen, as well as all the following photographers who chose to be a part of this project: Zoya Akulova, Algie Au, Matt Below, Margo Bors, Barry Breckling, Kyle Chamberlain, John Doyen, Barbara Eisenstein, Tom Elpel, Roger George, Tim Gladwin, Gary Gonzales, William Hartman, Mike Krebil, Bob Krumm, Louis-M. Landry, Jeff Martin, Steve Matson, Keir Morse, Jean Pawek, Jim Robertson, Vickie Shufer, Bob Sivinski, Vernon Smith, Robert Steers, Dr. Amadej Trnkoczy, Lily Jane Tsong, and Mary Winter. Thank you all!

INTRODUCTION

We owe a debt of gratitude to the generations of indigenous peoples of North America whose life and livelihood depended on plants for food and everything else. Much of this knowledge has been passed down generation to generation, and much has been rediscovered by researchers.

Many of the living "old ways" have been lost, but the knowledge of how to utilize the plants of the land has not been entirely forgotten. Various generations have realized the great value of knowing how to identify and use what nature has provided, even though this information waxes and wanes in importance in the general viewpoint.

When there is war or depression or famine, we desire to rekindle this link to our past, and hope for our future. When times are good, and money flows, we forget our roots. Just fifty years ago, you were considered poor, to be pitied, if you actually used wild foods.

With Euell Gibbons in the early 1970s, the tide began to turn again, and today everyone wants to know at least a little about our national heritage of wild foods. Many aware individuals want to be self-sufficient, and be a part of the solution. And today we have an abundance of books, videos, and classes to teach us about these skills.

In addition to the native flora, we now have an abundance of introduced plants and common edible weeds, which were used for generations throughout Europe and Asia. Sometimes these introduced flora are a blessing, sometimes not.

Scope of This Book

Foraging Idaho intends to cover plants that can be used primarily for food and are common in Idaho. We are not attempting to cover every single edible plant that could possibly be used for food, or those that are very marginal as food. Our focus is on those wild foods that are widespread, easily recognizable and identifiable, and can be used to create meals. Wild edibles that are too localized or only provide a marginal source of food are not included. Plants that are endangered or have the possibility of being endangered have not been included. In general, plants that are too easily confused with something poisonous have also been omitted. Mushrooms are not included.

The content of this book is intended to be useful for hikers and backpackers, and for anyone in urban and rural areas where so many of these plants still grow. Our goal is to provide a book that details the plants that a person attempting to live off the land would actually be eating.

If you embark on the study of ethnobotany, and start working closely with a mentor/teacher, your learning will expand way beyond the pages of this book, and that is how it should be.

This is not a book about medicinal properties, and though some medicinal aspects will be addressed in passing, we provide some ideal references at the end of this book.

Nor does this book focus on exclusively native plants. If you're hungry in the woods, or in your own backyard, you don't care if the plant is native or introduced, right?

We welcome your suggestions for additions to future editions.

Organization

The plants in this book are organized according to the system used by botanists.

Many books on plants organize the plants by flower color or environmental niche, both of which have their adherents and their pitfalls. This book categorizes plants according to their families, which gives you a broader perspective on the many more plants that are found in each botanical genus. As you will see, many of the genera (and some families) are entirely safe to use as food. This is how I was taught by my teacher and mentor, Dr. Leonid Enari, since he believed that, though there is no shortcut to learning about the identity and uses of plants, understanding the families will impart a far greater insight into the scope of "wild foods."

We'll start with the "lower" plants, then move on to the gymnosperms (the cone-bearing plants), then the flowering plants, in alphabetical order by their Latin family names.

PLANTS LISTED BY ENVIRONMENT TYPE

In our selection of plants for *Foraging Idaho*, we've attempted to include common edible plants from the different environments within the state.

Types of Environments in Idaho
We're listing the plants in this book only, and which environments where they can most likely be found. Some plants will be found in more than one environment.

Primary Types of Environments
According to biologists, Idaho is divided into the following eight regions. Starting from the north, there is the Panhandle region. Below that is the Clearwater Region. To the southeast of the Clearwater region is the Southwest Region, north, and below that, to the bottom of the state, is the Southwest Region, south. Immediately east of the Southwest Region, north, is the Salmon Region. Directly to the south—in the middle southern part of the state—is the Magic Valley region. Southeast of the Salmon Region is the Upper Snake region, and directly to the south is the Southeast Region.

In general, the ecological zones of Idaho are divided among the following six categories. "Urban," of course, is not an ecologic zone, per se, but certain plants described in this book are most likely to be found in the urban areas.

COOLER, MOISTER FOREST
Blackberry
Blueberry (*V. corymbosum,*
    V. oliginosum)
Bracken
Camas
Cherries
Crabapples
Hazelnut
High bush cranberry
Huckleberry
Kinnikinnick
Milkweed
Miner's Lettuce (*Claytonia sibirica*)
Mountain ash
Oregon Grape (*Mahonia nervosa*)
Rose
Rubus spp.
Serviceberry / Saskatoon
Sheep sorrel
Shooting star
Spring beauty
Strawberry
Sweet cicely
Violets
Wild ginger

HIGHER ELEVATIONS
American bistort
Avalanche Lily
Bracken
Brook Saxifrage
Camas (in meadows)
Cow Parsnip

Currant
Elderberry (*Sambucus racemosa melanocarpa*)
Fireweed
Huckleberry (*V. membranaceum*)
Kinnikinnick
Mountain Ash
Mountain Bluebells
Mountain sorrell
Pine
Raspberry
Serviceberry
Spring Beauty
Stinging Nettle
Strawberry
Thimbleberry
Thistle
Wild Onion

RIPARIAN
American Bistort
Blackberry (Rubus armeniacus and *R. discolor*)
Bracken
Brook Saxifrage
Burdock
Cattail
Cow parsnip
Crabapple
Grasses
Hazelnut
Hawthorne
Milkweed
Mint
Monkey flower
Mulberry
Nettle
nut sedge
Rush
Serviceberry
Shooting star

Strawberry
Veronica
Violet
Wapato
Watercress

WARMER, DRIER FORESTS
Mountain Forest /
Ponderosa Pine /
Interior Forest /
Cedar-Hemlock
Arrow Leaf Balsamroot
Biscuit Root
Bracken
Chokecherry
Crabapple
Currant
Elderberry (Blue)
Fireweed
Glacier lily
Harebells
Hazelnut
Hedge Mustard
Huckleberry
Kinnikinnick
Miner's Lettuce
Oregon Grape (*Mahonia repens*)
Pine
Prickly lettuce
Raspberry
Rubus sp.
Salsify
Sego lily
Serviceberry / Saskatoon
Spring Beauty
Stonecrop
Strawberry
Thimbleberry
Thistle
Violet
Yellowbell

Walnut
Waterleaf
Wild Onion
Wild Rose
Yampah

STEPPE / SAGEBRUSH STEPPE / JUNIPER STEPPE

Arrow Leaf Balsamroot
Biscuit Root
Bitterroot
Blueberry
Camas
Chokecherry
Currant, golden
Elder
Evening Primrose
Harebells
Hedge Mustard
Mustard
Oregon Grape (Berberis repens)
Prickly Pear cactus
Russian thistle
Salsify
Sego Lily
Serviceberry / Saskatoon
Stonecrop
Prickly lettuce
Thistle
Waterleaf
Wild Asparagus
Wild Onion
Yampah
Yellowbell

URBAN / DEVELOPED

Amaranth
Apple: Crabapple and Feral Domestic
   Apple
Bittercress
Blackberry

Black nightshade
Burdock
Carrot, wild
Chickweed
Chicory
Crabapple
Curly dock
Dandelion
Evening primrose
Filaree
Harebells
Hedge Mustard
Highbush cranberry
Lamb's-quarter
Mallow
Milkweed
Mint
Mountain ash
Mulberry
Mustard
Nut sedge
Oregon grape
Pine
Pineapple weed
Plantain
Prickly lettuce
Prunus sp.
Purslane
Russian thistle
Salsify
Sheep Sorrel
Shepherd's purse
Siberian elm
Stonecrop
Sow thistle
Stinging nettle
Thistle
Violet
Walnut
Wild asparagus
Wild rose

COLLECTING AND HARVESTING WILD FOODS

Since more and more people desire to learn how to "live off the land" and use wild plants for food and medicine, please practice sustainable collecting and harvesting methods.

The art (and science) of foraging is a sacred art, passed down generation to generation from the beginning of time. It is a fundamental skill, letting the fruits of the land feed you, as you in turn do everything you can to maintain the health and integrity of the land. People of the past instinctively knew that their survival was intimately tied to the health of the land. You could not overharvest, overgraze, and exploit without severe consequences. Remember: We and the land are One. It is an unfortunate point of modern days that this simple fact is being forgotten.

Always make sure it is both legal and safe for you to harvest wild foods. Legality can usually be determined simply by asking a few questions or making a phone call. In some cases, when dealing with public lands, the issue of legality may be a bit more difficult to ascertain.

You also want to be safe, making sure there are not agricultural or commercial toxins near the plants you intend to harvest. Again, it pays in the long run to carefully observe the surroundings and to ask a few questions.

Foraging has gotten more popular in the last few years for some very good reasons. People want to reconnect with their roots, and discover how our ancestors lived off the land. We're also discovering that wild foods not only taste good, but are generally far more nutritious than just about everything from the modern supermarket.

Be sure to set a good example both in how you forage, and in what you forage. Don't uproot plants if you don't need to. Don't overharvest from any area. And keep in mind that the landscape is overrun with invasive nonnatives, the so-called "weeds," mostly from Europe. There is usually a nearly unlimited amount of these plants, and you are usually welcome to collect these plants.

There has been some backlash recently by those who feel foragers are ruining the landscape. I would agree that in some very narrow instances, this has been the case—typically with mushroom collectors, and perhaps with wildcrafters of herbs for the resale market.

I implore you to develop a relationship with the plants, and learn how to harvest safely and sustainably. It is not that hard to be a conscientious forager, and in some cases you might actually see an increase in the number, size, and health of wild plants by your very careful thinning, pruning, and collecting. If you consider how the human race moved from forager to farmer, it was precisely through this careful and intimate relationship with the plants—benefiting both parties—that early farming methods developed.

Modern farming, far more than foraging, negatively affects vast swaths of native vegetation all over the globe, something we regard as a necessary aspect of food production. I strongly encourage you to learn more about how food is produced these days. Some good references are *Everything I Want to Do Is Illegal*, by Joel Salatin, and *In Defense of Food: An Eater's Manifesto*, by Michael Pollan. Both books give you a good picture of modern food production, the many problems associated with it, and some practical solutions—one of which is to eat wild foods!

Unless it is the root that you are using for food, you should never need to uproot a plant, especially if it is only the leaves that you intend to eat.

I have documented, in *Extreme Simplicity*, how I was able to extend the life of many annual weeds by carefully pinching back the leaves that I wanted to eat, and then allowing the plant to grow back before picking again. Even when I believe someone else will pull up the plant later, or plow the area, I still do not uproot the plants on general principle. If I leave the plant rooted, the root system is good for the soil and the plant continues to manufacture oxygen. Various insects and birds might eat the bugs on the plant, or its seeds. Let life continue.

When you are harvesting greens, snippers can be used, but usually nothing more is needed than your fingernails and maybe a sharp knife. Cut what you need, don't deplete an area, and move on.

Harvesting seeds is done when the plant is at the end of its annual cycle, but there is still no reason to uproot the plant. When I harvest curly dock or lamb's-quarter seed, I carefully try to get as much into my bag as possible. I know that some seed is being scattered, and that's a good thing for next season. I also know that a few seeds are still on the stalk, and that's a good thing for the birds in the area.

I nearly always harvest in an area of abundance. If there are very few specimens there, my usual course of action is to simply leave them alone.

You will note that I advise foragers to leave wild onions in the ground and to eat the greens. In cases of abundance, your thinning the roots will help stimulate more growth, and that is a good thing, akin to the passive agricultural practices of the Native Americans who once exclusively lived here in Idaho.

In general, foraging doesn't require many tools. You will need bags: plastic, cloth, paper, or whatever is appropriate for the food item. In some cases, you can harvest with buckets or tubs. Usually no other tools are needed, though I generally carry a Florian ratchet clipper for any cutting, and a knife or two. I rarely need a trowel, though it comes in handy with some harvesting.

The more you forage, the more you'll realize that your best tool is your memory. You'll learn to recognize where the mushrooms grow, where the berry vines are, and the fields that will be full of chickweed next spring. And the more you know, the less you'll need to carry.

HOW MUCH WILD FOOD IS OUT THERE, ANYWAY?

Plants Are Everywhere, but Not All Can Be Eaten

In his book *Participating in Nature*, Thomas Elpel created a unique chart, based on years of observation and analysis, to give a perspective on the sheer numbers of edible, medicinal, and poisonous plants. Elpel is also the author of *Botany in a Day*.

First, almost every plant with known ethnobotanical uses can be used medicinally; even some otherwise toxic plants can be used medicinally if you know the right doses and proper application. So, yes, medicine is everywhere. But nearly two-thirds of these plants are neither poisonous nor used for food for various reasons.

Extremely poisonous plants that will outright kill you are rare. In Idaho and surrounding states, for example, there is poison hemlock, which is somewhat easy to identify, and various toxic bulbs, such as death camas, which could be confused by a novice for something edible. Others that could cause death are various mushrooms, and certain commonly planted ornamentals. It is not uncommon to hear about mushroom sickness and even death.

Though only a few plants are deadly poisonous, many more can make you very sick, but would not normally kill you. Still, all the poisonous and toxic plants combined are just a very small percentage of all the known ethnobotanicals.

Edible plants comprise maybe a quarter of the known edible, medicinal, and poisonous plants. Of the plants we normally think of as "food plants," the overwhelming majority provide us primarily with greens. That is, throughout most of the year, the majority of the food you'll obtain from the wild consists

Edible, Medicinal, and Poisonous Plants

Poisonous Plants

Plants which are not poisonous, but which are not usually food, except as tea.

Edible Plants

Mildly Poisonous Plants
Very Poisonous Plants

Salad/Potherbs
Berries/Fruits
Starchy Roots
Seeds/Nuts

Medicinal Plants

of greens: food to make salads and stir-fries, and add to soups and vegetable dishes. These plants will not by themselves create a filling and balanced meal, but will add vitamins and minerals to your dried beans, MREs (meals ready-to-eat), freeze-dried camping food, and other foods. In general, greens are not high sources of protein, fats, or carbohydrates.

Berries and fruits comprise another category of wild foods. A small percentage of the wild foods you forage will be berries or fruits, and timing is everything. Unlike greens, which you can usually find year-round, fruits and berries are typically available only seasonally. If you want some during other times of the year, you'll need to dry them or make jams or preserves. This category includes blackberries, elderberries, mulberries, and many others. They provide sugar and flavor, but like greens, you would not make a meal entirely from fruits and berries.

An even smaller category of wild foods than berries consists of starchy roots, such as cattails and Jerusalem artichokes. These are great for energy, though they may not be available year-round. This is why these foods have traditionally been dried, and even powdered, and stored for use later in the year.

Another small category of wild foods consists of seeds and nuts. This includes grass seeds, pine nuts, and acorns, among many others. In this small category you obtain the carbohydrates, oils, and sometimes proteins that constitute the "staff of life." Though these are not available year-round, some have a longer harvest time than others. Some may have a harvest period as short as two weeks. Many grass seeds simply fall to the ground and are eaten by animals. Fortunately, most nuts and seeds can be harvested in season and stored for later use.

ARE WILD FOODS NUTRITIOUS?

It is a common misconception that "wild foods" are neither nutritious nor tasty. Both of these points are erroneous, as anyone who has actually taken the time to identify and use wild foods can testify. I've had many new students who were convinced about the nutritional value of wild foods, but assumed the plants nevertheless tasted bad. Of course, a bad cook can make even the best foods unpalatable. And if you pick wild foods and don't clean them, and don't use just the tender sections, and don't prepare them properly, you'll almost certainly turn people off to wild foods.

Wild foods are not only nutritious but can be as flavorful as any foods in the finest restaurants.

For your edification, here is a chart (pp. xxiii–xxiv) extracted from the US Department of Agriculture's (USDA's) *Composition of Foods* (also appears online) to give you an idea of the nutritional content of the common wild foods.

Nutritional Composition of Wild Foods (per 100 grams, unless otherwise indicated)

Blanks denote no data available; dashes denote lack of data for a constituent believed to be present in measurable amounts. Only a select number of plants for which we have data are represented. Primary source: *Composition of Foods*, US Department of Agriculture

Plant	Calories	Protein (g)	Fat (g)	Calcium (mg)	Phosphorus (mg)	Iron (mg)	Sodium (mg)	Potassium (mg)	Vitamin A (IU)	Thiamine (mg)	Riboflavin (mg)	Niacin (mg)	Vit. C (mg)	Part
Amaranth	36	3.5	0.5	267	67	3.9	—	411	6,100	0.08	0.16	1.4	80	Leaf, raw
Carob	45	4.5		352	81	2.9	35	827	14		0.4	1.89	0.2	Pods
Cattail		8%	2%											Rhizomes
Chia seed		20.2%		631	860	7.72	16	407	54	0.62	0.17	8.8	1.6	Seed
CHICORY TRIBE														
Chicory	20	1.8	0.3	86	40	0.9	—	420	4,000	0.06	0.1	0.5	22	Leaf, raw
Dandelion	45	2.7	0.7	187	66	3.1	76	397	14,000	0.19	0.26	—	35	Leaf, raw
Sow thistle	20	2.4	0.3	93	35	3.1	—	—	2,185	0.7	0.12	0.4	5	Leaf, raw
Chickweed														
Dock	28	2.1	0.3	66	41	1.6	5	338	12,900	0.09	0.22	0.5	119	Leaf, raw
Fennel	28	2.8	0.4	100	51	2.7	—	397	3,500	—	—	—	31	Leaf, raw
Filaree	—	2.5	—	—	—	—	—	—	7,000	—	—	—	—	Leaf
Grass										300–500 IU	2,000 to 2,800 IU		300 to 700 mg	Leaf, raw
Jerusalem artichoke	75	2.3	0.1	14	78	3.4	-	-	20	0.2	0.06	1.3	4	Root, raw
Lamb's-quarter	43	4.2	0.8	309	72	1.2	43	452	11,600	0.16	0.44	1.2	80	Leaf, raw
Mallow	37	4.4	0.6	249	69	12.7	—	—	2,190	0.13	0.2	1.0	35	Leaf
Milkweed	—	0.8	0.5		—	—	—	—	—	—	—	—	—	Leaf
Miner's lettuce						10% RDA			22% RDA				33% RDA	Leaf
MUSTARD FAMILY														
Mustard	31	3	0.5	183	50	3	32	377	7,000	0.12	0.22	0.8	97	Leaf
Shepherd's purse	33	4.2	0.5	208	86	4.8	—	394	1,554	0.08	0.17	0.4	36	Leaf
Watercress	19	2.2	0.3	120	60	0.2	41	330	3,191		0.12	0.2	43	Leaf

Plant	Calories	Protein (g)	Fat (g)	Calcium (mg)	Phosphorus (mg)	Iron (mg)	Sodium (mg)	Potassium (mg)	Vitamin A (IU)	Thiamine (mg)	Riboflavin (mg)	Niacin (mg)	Vit. C (mg)	Part
Nasturtium														
Nettle	65	5.5	0.7	481	71	1.64	4	334	2,011	—	0.16	0.38	76	Leaf
New Zealand spinach	19	2.2	0.3	58	46	2.6	159	795	4,300	0.04	0.17	0.6	30	Leaf, raw
Oak (acorn flour)	65% carbohydrates	6%	18%	43	103	1.21	0	712	51	0.1	0.1	2.3	0	Nut
ONION FAMILY														
Chives	28	1.8	0.3	69	44	1.7	—	250	5,800	0.08	0.13	0.5	56	Leaf, raw
Garlic	137	6.2	0.2	29	202	1.5	19	529	—	0.25	0.08	0.5	15	Clove, raw
Onion	36	1.5	0.2	51	39	1	5	231	2,000	0.05	0.05	0.4	32	Young leaf, raw
Passion fruit [per pound]				31	151	3.8	66	831	1,650				71	Fruit
Pine nuts	635	12	60.5		604	5.2				1.28				Nut
Prickly pear	42	0.5	0.1	20	28	0.3	2	166	60	0.01	0.03	0.4	22	Fruit, raw
Purslane	21	30	1.7	0.4	103	39	3.5	—	—	2,500	0.03	0.1	0.5	Leaf & stem, raw
Rose	162	1.6		169	61	1.06	4	429	4,345		0.16	1.3	426	Fruit, raw
SEAWEED														
Dulse	—	—	3.2	296	267	—	2,085	8,060	—	—	—	—	—	Leaf
Irish moss	—	—	1.8	885	157	8.9	2,892	2,844	—	—	—	—	—	Leaf
Kelp	—	—	1.1	1,093	240	—	3,007	5,273	—	—	—	—	—	Leaf

Ferns

There are thirteen families of ferns. According to Dr. Leonid Enari, the young, uncurling, growing tips of all ferns are edible, and taste a bit nutty. These have long been steamed and served with butter or cheese, or mixed into various vegetable dishes.

You will encounter many ferns in Idaho and beyond, aside from what we have presented here. A few have a long history of use as food.

BRACKEN FAMILY (DENNSTAEDTIACEAE)

Among the ferns, the Bracken family contains about eleven genera and about 170 species. Its only representative in Idaho is the bracken, or brake fern.

Bracken leaf. RICK ADAMS

BRACKEN
Pteridium aquilinum

Use: Young uncurling shoots used for food
Range: Throughout the state, mostly in the shady areas of the mountains and canyons; not found in the deserts
Similarity to toxic species: See Cautions.
Best time: Spring
Status: Somewhat common in the correct terrain
Tools needed: Clippers

Properties

Bracken can apparently be found worldwide, and all throughout the United States. In Idaho, bracken can be found throughout the state, in pastures, on hillsides, in wooded areas, and even in full sun. You'll find it most commonly on the north, shady sides of hillsides or on shady hillsides where water seeps and where little sun gets through the canopy of whatever larger trees grow there.

The rhizomes are hairy and sprawling underground, sometimes branching. The petiole is black near the base, with dense brown hairs. The plants grow from 1 to 4 feet tall, and the overall appearance of each frond is roughly triangular; each is twice-pinnately divided.

Uses

The young shoots are the edible portion and they have the appearance of the head of a fiddle, which is where the common name "fiddlehead" comes from. The young shoots will uncurl and grow into the full fern fronds. The fiddleheads are picked when young and could be eaten raw or cooked. I like to toss a few in salads when fiddleheads are in season; they impart a nutty flavor.

Bracken fiddlehead. BARBARA KOLANDER

More commonly, these are boiled or steamed and served with butter or cheese. They are easy to recognize and have gained a resurgence of popularity as more people are rediscovering wild foods. Bracken is also a good vegetable to add to soups and stews, and mixed dishes.

Just carefully pinch off the tender unfolding top, and you can gently rub off the hair. Use as a nibble or cook. Do not eat the fully opened ferns.

Cautions

Researchers have identified a substance called ptaquiloside in bracken fern, a known carcinogen. So is it safe to eat? It has been a food staple of Native Americans for centuries, if not millennia, and the Japanese also enjoy bracken and consider it one of the delicacies of spring. Although actual scientific data is inconclusive, there is a higher rate of intestinal cancer among Native Americans and the Japanese, and this could be linked to the use of bracken fern. Livestock have been known to be mildly poisoned by eating quantities of the raw bracken ferns. According to Dr. James Adams, you should "boil the fiddleheads to get rid of as much ptaquiloside as possible."

A small fiddlehead. RICK ADAMS

There are many who are not so concerned about such inconclusive studies. For example, Steven Brill, in his *Identifying and Harvesting Edible and Medicinal Plants*, states, "I wouldn't be afraid of eating reasonable quantities of wild [bracken] fiddleheads during their short season." Another forager, Green Deane, says, "I am willing to risk a few fiddleheads with butter once or twice a spring, which is about as often as I can collect enough in this warm place."

The final choice is up to you. For perspective, we regularly hear things far worse than the above about coffee, high-fructose corn syrup, sugar, and french fries, yet people seem to have no problem purchasing and eating these substances. That doesn't make them good for you, but eating some in moderation is not likely to be the sole cause of cancer or other illness.

Dr. Enari (my mentor and holder of doctorate degrees in chemistry and botany) regarded the entire group of

Edible fiddleheads of bracken. LILY JANE TSONG

Young bracken. RICK ADAMS

ferns as safe for food, though he added that he knew of none that were toxic if you abide by the following precautions. Cook all fiddleheads that you intend to eat, since some may be a bit toxic raw. He advised cleaning fiddleheads of hairs, if any, before cooking. Dr. Enari also advised to not eat any mature fern fronds. Though many may be safe when mature, they are not as palatable as the young fiddlehead. You need to get to know that individual fern before you eat its mature fronds. Otherwise, eat only the fiddleheads, clean them of hairs, and cook them before eating.

Others I spoke to in preparing this book told me that they would be much more conservative regarding the edibility of all fern fiddleheads, and would only eat those species that have been identified as edible.

Lewis and Clark
Meriwether Lewis wrote about the bracken fern on January 22, 1806: "There are three species of fern in this neighbourhood the root one of which the natves eat; this grows very abundant in the open uplands and praries . . . the center of the root is divided into two equal parts by a strong flat & white ligament like a piece of thin tape—on either side of this there is a white substance which when the root is roasted in the embers is much like wheat dough and not very unlike it in flavour, though it has also a pungency which becomes more visible after you have chewed it some little time; this pungency was disagreeable to me, but the natives eat it very voraciously and I have no doubt but it is a very nutricious food."

Some Other Fern Groups

The Wood Fern family (Dryopteridaceae) consists of about 40 to 45 genera, four local genera, and more than 1,600 species worldwide. This family includes *Dryopteris* spp., consisting of about one hundred species worldwide and commonly called wood fern. The family also includes *Polystichum* spp., with about 175 species worldwide and commonly referred to as sword fern.

The Cliff Fern family (Woodsiaceae) consists of fifteen genera and about 700 species worldwide. One species sometimes eaten is lady fern (*Athyrium filix-femina*) and two varieties.

The Deer Fern family (Blechnaceae) consists of nine genera and about 250 species worldwide. Common locally, and sometimes eaten, is deer fern (*Blechum spicant*).

Gymnosperms

This is a class of plants whose seeds are formed in cones. Gymnosperm means "naked seed" because the seeds are exposed, or not encased, such as the Angiosperms, whose seeds are enclosed in an ovary. This group includes all conifers (such as pines), the unique ginkgo biloba, and some others.

PINE FAMILY (PINACEAE)

A view of pine needles and cones. RICK ADAMS

PINE
Pinus spp.

Use: Needles for tea and spice; nuts for food
Range: Various species are found in the mountains and throughout the state. Often planted in urban areas.
Similarity to toxic species: None
Best time: Nuts in the fall; needles can be collected anytime.
Status: Common in certain localities
Tools needed: Clippers for needles

Properties
Pines are fairly widespread trees, with some preferring burned-over areas. The Pine family is said to supply about half the world's lumber needs. The family consists of ten genera and 193 species. There are ninety-four species of *Pinus* in the Northern Hemisphere, and at least eight are known to grow in the wild in Idaho. The best pine nuts in Idaho are *Pinus monophyla* (single needle pinyon), *P. flexis* (limber pine), and the threatened *P. albicaulis* (white bark pine). In Idaho and surrounding area, we find *Pinus contorta* with needles mostly in 2s; western yellow pine (*P. ponderosa*) with needles mostly in 3s; *P. flexis* (needles in 5s, mostly in the east), *P. albicaulis* (needles in 5s); and western white pine (*P. monticola*) with needles in 5s.

Pines are one of the easier conifers to identify: All the needles are "bundled" at their base into groups of one to five with papery sheaths; each such cluster is called a fascicle.

The pines in Idaho can range from about 30 feet tall (the lodgepole pine) up to about 200 feet tall (the western yellow pine). Look for the bundled needles and look for the cones. The cones are often tightly spiraled with a variety of scale types. As the cones mature, they open up to reveal a pine nut under each scale. Each pine nut has a thin black shell and an oily white inside.

Uses

Though there are a few *potential* foods with the pines, it is mostly the seeds that will provide you with food that is both substantial and palatable.

The cones mature and open in the fall. As the scales open sufficiently, the seeds drop to the ground, where they can be collected if you're there at the right time and beat the animals to them. The seeds may drop over a two-week to a month-long period. One of the best methods to harvest is to lay sheets under the trees to catch the seeds so they're not lost in the grass. The seeds can then be shelled and eaten as a snack, added to soups, or mashed and added to biscuits or pancakes.

I have taken the not-fully-mature cones and put them into a fire, carefully watching them so they don't burn. The idea is to open the scales and then get the seeds. However, I do not recommend this method.

The tender needles can also be collected and brewed into a tea. Put the needles in a covered container, and boil at a low temperature for a few minutes. The tea is rich in vitamin C and very aromatic and tasty—that is, if you enjoy the flavor of a Christmas tree, which is what you'll smell like after drinking it. It's very good.

Yes, we have all heard of eating the cambium layer of pine trees. I regard this as a "survival food," meaning it could be worth all the work involved if you're actually near-starving, but it also depends on the species of pine whose cambium you are collecting, the location, and time of year. Others have had more positive experiences with this food source.

Botanist William Schlegel adds, "Salish ate the inner bark of *Pinus ponderosa* at about the same time they harvested *Lewisia rediviva*. It was a very important source of sugar and vitamins at that time of the year. Northern Rockies ponderosa is a little more like Jeffrey pine in California but it still tastes like turpentine.

FORAGER NOTE: Some of the very long needles of certain pines are excellent for coiled baskets.

Sugary turpentine might be a hard sell for modern taste buds. Travelers' Rest State Park in Montana still has living ponderosas with bark harvest scars. The practice as done by the Montana Salish didn't kill the trees but did gradually fill them with pitch, and the stumps of these trees provide a potent fire starter long after. The cambium was eaten only fresh, and the main problem in my view is the turpentine flavor. I wonder if even in a survival situation we would need this food in modern times. It's entirely possible that introduced plants since that time (such as asparagus and apples) might eclipse the pine's cambium both as a spring vegetable (asparagus) and as a sugar source (apples)."

Eudicots

This category was formerly referred to as dicots. The sprouts begin with two cotyledons, and the flower parts generally occur in 4s or 5s. All families in this category are arranged alphabetically by their Latin names.

MUSKROOT FAMILY (ADOXACEAE)

This family has five genera and about 200 species worldwide. Only two of the genera are represented in Idaho, *Sambucus* and *Viburnum*.

Elderberry fruits.

ELDERBERRY
Sambucus spp.

There are twenty species of *Sambucus* worldwide. There are three species of *Sambucus* in Idaho. The blue elderberry is *S. nigra* ssp. *caerulea* (sometimes known as *S. caerulea*), which is widespread. The black elderberry is *S. racemosa* var. *melanocarpa*, also widespread. The red-fruiting species is *S. racemosa* var. *racemosa*.

Use: Flowers for tea and food; berries for "raisins"; jam and jelly; juice
Range: Throughout the state in the mountains, on the urban fringe, and generally in most environments
Similarity to toxic species: See Cautions.
Best time: Spring for flowers; summer for fruit
Status: Common
Tools needed: Clippers for flowers; clippers and a good, sturdy bucket for berries

A view of the elderberry's flower cluster, fruit cluster, and leaf. HELEN W. NYERGES

David Martinez examines the ripe Mexican elder fruit.

Elderberry.

FORAGER NOTE: If you don't want your fruit to get all smashed and crushed, don't collect in a bag. Collect in a basket or bucket, and don't pack too many into the bucket.

Properties

Elder trees can be found throughout the United States, and throughout Idaho. They prefer drier regions, as well as along streams, and in the higher mountain regions. They are generally small trees, with oppositely arranged, pinnately divided leaves with a terminal leaflet. Each leaflet has a fine serration along its edge.

The plant is often inconspicuous, but is very obvious when it blossoms in spring, with its many yellowish-white flower clusters. By early summer, the fruits develop in clusters, which are often drooping from the weight.

Uses

Remember: Black and blue is good for you; red as a brick will get you sick! (A Boy Scout saying.)

The blue berries, rich in vitamin A, with fair amounts of potassium and calcium, can be eaten raw or can be mashed and blended with applesauce for

---

RECIPE

Elderberry Sauce

This simple sauce goes well with any game (such as duck), but feel free to try it with chicken too!

1 pound elderberries (freeze the clusters first, crush them lightly with your hands, and the berries will fall off easily)

1 large sweet onion or 7–8 scallions

⅔ cup red wine vinegar

¾ cup sugar or honey

1 teaspoon grated ginger

A couple of cloves

½ teaspoon of salt, or to taste

Place the berries in a pot and squeeze them with your hand to release the juice. Place all the other ingredients in the pot and bring to a boil for 10 minutes, then strain the liquid through a sieve.

Return the liquid to the pot, bring to a simmer, and reduce until you have achieved the right consistency (like a commercial steak sauce). You can prepare it in advance and keep it in the fridge for many days.

—RECIPE FROM PASCAL BAUDAR

a unique dessert, especially if you are using wild apples. The berries can also be used for making wines, jellies, jams, and pies.

Though some of the Indian tribes of the Northwest ate the red berries when cooked, there are people today who get sick from the red ones. I do not advise that you eat red elderberries at all; however, if you decide to try them, cook them well and sample only a little bit at first to see how your body reacts.

Wild-food researcher Pascal Baudar likes to dry and powder the blue fruit, and sprinkle it over ice cream. The whole flower cluster can be gathered, dipped in batter, and fried, producing a wholesome pancake. Try dipping the flower clusters in a batter of the sweet yellow cattail pollen (see Cattail, p. 234) and frying it like pancakes. It's delicious!

Another method to use with the flowers is to remove them from the clusters and the little stems, and then mix with flour in a proportion of 50/50 for baking pastries, breads, biscuits, and more. The flowers also make a traditional Appalachian tea that was said to be useful for colds, fevers, and headaches.

The long, straight stems of elder have a soft pith and have historically been hollowed out and used for such things as pipe stems, blowguns, flutes, and straws for stoking a fire.

Cautions

Be sure to cook the fruit before eating it, and avoid the red berries entirely. While not everyone will get sick from eating the dark purple or black berries raw, they can cause severe nausea in some people. Therefore, cook all fruit before using for drinks or other dishes.

Do not consume the leaves as this will result in sickness.

HIGHBUSH CRANBERRY
Viburnum edule

There are about 200 species worldwide of *Viburnum*, and at least three identified in Idaho: *V. edule* (aka *V. opulus* var. *edule*), found mostly in the northern part of the state and called squashberry or highbush cranberry; *V. opulus* var. *americanum*, also called American bush cranberry or cranberry tree; and *V. opulus* var. *opulus*, also called highbush cranberry. None of these are related to the common cranberry, which is *Vaccinium macrocarpon*, native to the eastern United States and commonly cultivated.

Use: The fruits are eaten.

Range: Found from Alaska to Newfoundland, and south to northern Oregon and Idaho. The native species is found in moist cool woods and swamps.

Similarity to toxic species: None

Best time: Flowers from May–July, with the fruit following in late summer

Status: Common

Tools needed: A collecting basket

Properties

These are deciduous, semi-erect shrubs that can get up to 10 feet tall, but are usually around 4 to 5 feet tall. The opposite leaves are petiolate, palmately veined, and shallowly three-lobed, appearing somewhat like a currant leaf. Sometimes you'll see some unlobed leaves. Each leaf is sharply toothed, usually 3 to 10 centimeters long and wide, with a pair of glandular projections near the junction with the petiole. The leaves turn conspicuously red in the fall, and by winter, the leaves fall off. The white flowers are formed in compound umbels. Each corolla is widely bell-shaped, whitish, with five lobes. The fruit is a one-seeded drupe, and matures to a bright red or orange.

A view of the fruit and the leaf of *V. opulus.*
DR. AMADEJ TRNKOCZY

The fruit and leaf of *V. opulus.* ZOYA AKULOVA

Uses

When you encounter this semi-erect shrub, you will be inclined to taste a fruit if in season. Chew on it and spit out the seed, and maybe you'll like it, maybe you won't. I've heard the flavor described as musky, but let's just say it is unique. Cooking the fruits to make a jam or jelly will mellow the flavor, and most people enjoy it at that point. I used to nibble on the raw fruit, but I prefer making a jam or juice from it. I do this by mashing the ripe fruits, pouring them through a sieve, and then gently cooking the juice and sweetening it if I just want a juice. We've also cooked the fruit down and used it as a pie filling. You could also simply mix highbush cranberry fruit with other wild or domestic fruits for juices, jams, pie fillings, etc.

Fruits from the often-cultivated *Viburnum opulus* tend to be more bitter. The native *Viburnum edule* tends to be sweeter. Fruits that are left on the bush into the winter will be a bit mellower and tasty raw.

AMARANTH FAMILY (AMARANTHACEAE)

The Amaranth family has seventy-five genera and 900 species worldwide. Of the members of the *Amaranthus* genus in Idaho, *A. retroflexus* seems to be the most common of about six species.

AMARANTH
Amaranthus spp.

Use: Seeds for soup or pastries and bread products; leaves can be eaten raw or cooked

Range: Amaranth is widespread. Though it is most common in the disturbed soils of farms, gardens, fields, and urban lots, you can usually find some amaranth in open areas where there is some moisture, even seasonally.

Similarity to toxic species: Some ornamentals resemble amaranth. Some toxic plants superficially resemble amaranth, such as the nightshades (e.g., *Solanum nigrum*, whose raw leaves could make you sick). Individual jimsonweed leaves (*Datura* spp.) have been confused for amaranth leaves.

Rick Adams next to a tall seeding amaranth.

Generally, once amaranth begins to flower and go to seed, this confusion is diminished.

Best time: Spring for the leaves; late fall for the seeds

Status: Common

Tools needed: Tightly woven bag for collecting the seeds

Properties

Though there are many species of *Amaranthus*, *A. retroflexus* is most common in Idaho.

Amaranth is an annual. The ones with erect stalks can grow up to 3 feet and taller, depending on the species. Some are more branched and are lower to the ground. When young, the root of one of the common varieties, *A. retroflexus*, is red, and the bottoms of the young leaves are purple. The leaves of *A. retroflexus* are oval-shaped, alternate, and glossy. Other *Amaranthus* leaves can be ovate to linear.

A view of the young red *Amaranthus retroflexus* root.

The plant produces flowers, but they are not conspicuous. They are formed in spike-like clusters, and numerous shiny black seeds develop when the plant matures in late summer. The plant is common and widespread in urban areas, fields, farms, backyards, and roadsides.

Uses

Amaranth is a versatile plant, with edible parts available throughout its growing season.

The young leaves and tender stems of late winter and spring can be eaten raw in salads, but because there is often a hint of bitterness, they are best mixed with other greens. Young and tender stems are boiled in many parts

A. retroflexus. Note red root. RICK ADAMS

of the world and served with butter or cheese as a simple vegetable. Older leaves get bitter and should be boiled into a spinach-like dish, or added to soups, stews, stir-fries, etc. In Mexico, leaves are sometimes dried and made into a flour, which is added to tamales and other dishes.

A. retroflexus leaves. RICK ADAMS

Amaranth begins to produce seeds in late summer, and once the seeds are black, they can be harvested. The entire plant is generally already very withered and dried up by the time you're harvesting seeds. The seeds are added to soups, bread batter, and pastry products.

The seeds and leaves are very nutritious; no doubt part of the reason this plant was so revered in the old days. One hundred grams of the seed contains about 358 calories, 247 milligrams (mg) of calcium, 500 mg of phosphorus, and 52.5 mg of potassium. The seed offers a nearly complete balance of essential amino acids, including lysine and methionine.

The leaf is also very nutritious, being high in calcium, and potassium. One hundred grams (about ½ cup) of amaranth leaf has 267–448 mg of calcium, 411–617 mg of potassium, 53–80 mg of vitamin C, 4,300 micrograms (mcg) of beta-carotene, and 1,300 mcg of niacin. This volume of leaf contains about 35 calories.

Historical note: The seed and leaf of this plant played a key part of the diet in precolonial Mexico. The seeds were mixed with honey or blood and shaped into images of gods, and these images were then eaten as a "communion." Sound familiar? After the Spanish invaded Mexico, they made it illegal to grow the amaranth plant, with the justification that it was a part of "pagan rituals."

FORAGER NOTE: Amaranths are a diverse group. Some have an erect stalk, some are highly branched, and some are prostrate.

CARROT (OR PARSLEY) FAMILY (APIACEAE)

The Carrot family has about 300 genera worldwide, with about 3,000 species. In Idaho, there are over thirty genera of this family. Many are cultivated for food, spice, and medicine, but some are highly toxic. Never eat anything that looks carrot- or parsley-like if you haven't positively identified it.

WILD CARROT
Daucus carota

A patch of wild carrots.

There are about twenty species of *Daucus* worldwide, and two are found in Idaho.

Use: The roots can be dug and used like farm-grown carrots, but they are tougher. Seeds are sometimes used as a spice.

Range: Not a native, but can be found throughout much of Idaho, often in disturbed or poor soils and along roadsides

Similarity to toxic species: See Cautions.

Best time: For a more tender root, dig before the plant flowers.

Status: Found sporadically throughout the Northwest

Tools needed: Shovel

Properties

If you've ever grown carrots in your garden, you will recognize the wild carrot in the wild, except it will typically be smaller. Smell the crushed leaf, and scrape a bit of the root and smell it. Does it smell like carrot? The root of the wild carrot is white, not orange, and if you scratch it, you'll get that very characteristic carrot aroma.

The leaves are pinnately dissected, with the leaflet segments linear to lanceolate—just like the leaves of a garden carrot. The flowers are formed in umbels of white flowers, with a tiny central flower that is purple. As the umbel matures, it closes up and has the appearance of a bird's nest.

Uses

The roots can be dug, washed, and eaten like garden carrots, though they are usually tough. This was one of the first wild foods that I learned to use. It was always a feeling of great mystery and pleasure to dig into a wild field and pull up one of these white

Note the tiny purple flower in the middle of the carrot inflorescence. ALGIE AU

roots. Was it a farm carrot gone feral? Probably. It still woke up some inner distant memory of "hunter-gatherer."

Sometimes, I simply peel the outer part of the taproot and discard the very tough inner core. I then wash the outer layer of the root, chop or slice it, and add it to raw or cooked foods.

The entire root might be tender if it's growing in moist and rich soil. In this case it can be sliced thin and added to salads. These roots are probably best added to soups, stews, and various cooked dishes.

But most of the roots I've found are pretty tough, and only the outer layer can be eaten. I slice this thin and cook it. It adds a good flavor to soups, though it lacks the carotene of commercial carrots.

The seeds of the mature plant can be collected and used as a seasoning, to taste.

The whitish root of the wild carrot. ALGIE AU

Cautions

The Carrot family contains some very good food and spices. However, make absolutely certain that you have a carrot and not poison hemlock, which are both members of this family. The wild carrot plant has that very distinctive carrot aroma, and has fine hairs on the stalk. Poison hemlock lacks the hairs and usually you will see mottled purple markings on the stem.

FORAGER NOTE: When young, poison hemlock resembles Italian parsley, and looks very much like the wild carrot as it grows taller. If uncertain, here are some tips: Rub a leaf and smell the aroma. Does it smell like carrot? Then it probably is. Does it smell musky, like dust or old socks? It's probably poison hemlock. Look at the mature stalk. If you see purple blotches, you have poison hemlock. Look at the flower umbel. Is there a single purple flower in the middle? If so, you have a wild carrot. Remember, never eat any wild plant until you have positively identified it.

A view of the parsley-like poison hemlock leaf.

The purple blotches of the lower stalk of poison hemlock.

COW PARSNIP
Heracleum maximum, formerly *H. lanatum*

There are about eighty species of *Heracleum* worldwide; two species are found in Idaho.

Use: The tender parts of the stalk are edible.
Range: Prefers lowlands and moist environments. Can also be found in higher elevations.
Similarity to toxic species: See Cautions.
Best time: Spring
Status: Somewhat common
Tools needed: Knife

Properties
This is a robust plant, an obvious member of the Carrot or Parsley family because of its white flowers clustered in umbels. The flowers are composed of five sepals, five petals, five stamens, and one pistil.

The plant can grow up to 10 feet tall, though 4 to 6 feet seems to be the norm. It produces leaves with three large, coarsely toothed lobes, very much palmate, almost like maple leaves. The plant has a stout, hollow stalk. There is also a carrot-like taproot.

The plant is most commonly found in mountain meadows and moist areas. It's a typically conspicuous plant, which you cannot help but notice.

Uses
The tender stalk can be peeled and eaten raw, though it is really better when you cook it. The young stalks are best, and the flavor is often compared to celery.

The dried and powdered leaves have been used as a seasoning for other foods, generally as you'd use salt. You can experiment and see if this appeals to you. The leaves have also been dried and burned, and the ash used as a seasoning.

Native Americans of the area had many uses for the cow parsnip plant, besides eating the young peeled stems. They would make the plant into a poultice to treat sores and bruises. The hollow stems were also used as drinking straws, as well as flutes.

Cautions
Although this is one of the easiest members of the Carrot family to identify, the family does contain some deadly members, so do not eat any part of this plant until you've made positive identification.

Also, the young stalk is typically peeled before eating because the surface of the stalk causes a dermatitis reaction in some people.

Close-up of the cow parsnip stem.
ZOYA AKULOVA

The cow parsnip plant in flower. BOB SIVINSKI

BISCUIT-ROOT
Lomatium spp.

There are about seventy-five species of *Lomatium* worldwide and forty-two in Idaho. There are many named subspecies.

A view of the biscuit root plant. MARY WINTER

Use: All parts of the plant are edible, though the roots are most commonly eaten. Some species are unpalatable.
Range: Widespread; can be found up into Canada, and south to California
Similarity to toxic species: See Cautions.
Best time: The most responsible and rewarding time to gather roots is when the plants have developed mature seed (sometimes as early as March or April). But since the above-ground parts of the plant desiccate and vanish early in the summer, the optimal harvest window is brief. Plants harvested in the late flowering stage may have accumulated enough carbohydrates to be worthwhile.
Status: Widespread; found in seasonally arid habitats, on ridgetops, open slopes, lava flats, and in open meadows

Tools needed: A sharpened stick, or steel pry bar, is a more effective and less destructive harvesting tool than a trowel (these plants lodge themselves in very stony soils). Gloves prevent many scraped knuckles.

Properties

These plants have a taproot that is usually short and tuberous-thickened, irregularly shaped, and occasionally slender and elongate. The stems tend to be prostrate and creeping, rarely rising higher than knee-height. Leaves are typically pinnately dissected (or alternately dissected), with the individual leaflets being thread-like to wide. Leaves are usually all basal, but there may be one or more cauline leaves. Different species can have white, yellow, or purple flowers. The inflorescence is a compound umbel, which matures into seeds with flattened backs and wings.

With a bit of fieldwork, you'll be able to recognize a *Lomatium*, though it may take a bit longer to learn to recognize the different species.

Uses

Lomatium and *Cymopterus* are diverse genera. The roots, young flower stalks, and leaves vary in palatability, according to species. The less palatable species, like *L. dissectum*, have powerful medicinal uses. Indigenous harvesters have focused on a few species that have either large, pleasantly flavored roots or tender stems (often called "Indian celery"). In the Intermountain West, there is usually some edible *Lomatium* at hand, though most species have slender roots and are strongly parsley-flavored.

While the root may be eaten raw, cooking improves appeal. Biscuit-root is a versatile staple, appreciated by diverse indigenous cultures. There are innumerable traditional processing methods and recipes. Biscuit-root can be boiled, mashed, roasted, or fried, like potatoes or parsnips. Biscuit-root is particularly amenable to drying, with or without peeling, whole or mashed into cakes. Dried roots can be crushed into a flour, which can be reconstituted into dough, and shaped to form dried "pinch cakes" that may include other dry ingredients. Boiling and blending with fat was a popular way of serving fresh or dried biscuit-root. Peeling with the thumbnail can be made easier by rubbing or gently knocking a sackful of roots against a hard surface. Dried biscuit-root was a common provision and trade item for carb-craving salmon cultures. *Lomatiums* are perennial plants, which require years to grow to a harvestable size. They are culturally vital, and still harvested by native people. Respectful harvest of biscuit-root keeps in mind their locally fragile but geographically extensive nature. Digging disturbance may perpetuate certain native foods, particularly where sod competes, but always leave the majority of plants to seed future abundance. Sampling sensitive indigenous foods is most appropriate in educational

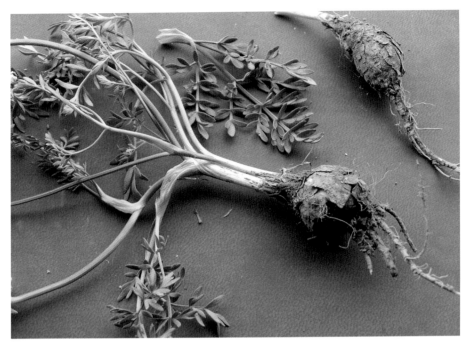

A view of the root of the biscuit root. MARY WINTER

contexts, which instill appreciation for native cultures and ecologies. Such sampling needs to be occasional and limited, to keep populations healthy. Weedy biennial root vegetables, abundant in places disturbed by the colonizing civilization, provide ample daily fare for modern foragers.

The staple species used by native groups (*L. canbyi*, *L. cous*) have a mild flavor, similar to parsnips. Other species have a harsh aromatic flavor reminiscent of strong parsley or even kerosene. Drying and/or boiling may ameliorate harsh flavors. The parsley-like flavor can be difficult to complement in dishes, but it blends superbly with mustard. The tender young "celery" stems of taller species (*L. nudicaule*, *L. triternatum*) were relished among the earliest fresh vegetables of spring. The leaves are some of the earliest to sprout in sagebrush country. They can be used like parsley for a garnish, raw or cooked.

The papery seeds are best if collected before the plant begins to dry up. These can be added to other foods as a spice. Seeds from more aromatic species were used like mothballs and traded as a commodity.

Cautions

Because the deadly poison hemlock and water hemlock are in this same family, with the same floral structure, you must be absolutely certain you are correctly identifying biscuit-root if you intend to eat it. There are several significant differences between biscuit-root and poison hemlock. Poison hemlock can grow to 7 feet tall, with luxuriant leaves and stout stems blotched with purple as the plant matures. Unlike moisture-loving hemlocks, biscuit-root species grow in soils subject to extremes of aridity and exposure. Biscuit-roots are compact plants, often ubiquitous in upland habitats, and very distinctive in their hardy adaptation. The differences between these plants become comfortably clear with familiarity.

Lewis and Clark

This was one of the most important plants for Native Americans of the Columbia River drainage. Speaking of *Lomatium cous*, known as "cous" or "cows," Lewis wrote what he observed of the Nez Perce, then called Chopunnish. On May 9, 1806, Lewis wrote, "among other roots those called by them the Quawmash [camas] and Cows [cous biscuit-root] are esteemed the most agreeable and valuable as they are also the most abundant. The cows is a knobbed root of an irregularly rounded form not unlike the Gensang [American ginseng] in form and consistence. This root they collect, rub off a thin black rhind which covers it and pounding it expose it in cakes to the sun. these [cous] cakes ate [at] about an inch and ¼ thick and 6 by 18 in width, when dryed they either eat this bread alone without any further preparation, or boil it and make a thick muselage; the latter is most common and much the most agreeable. The flavor of this root is not very unlike the gensang—this [cous] root they collect as early as the snows disappear in the spring . . ."

Later, Lewis relates how a captain was given some dried camas roots as a present. Lewis writes, "but in our estimation those of cows [*Lomatium cous*] are much better, I am confident they are much more healthy. The men . . . obtained a good store of roots and bread."

SWEET CICELY
Osmorhiza berteroi, O. occidentalis

There are about ten species of *Osmorhiza* worldwide; in Idaho, there are four recorded species.

Use: Roots used as a snack and as a seasoning
Range: In wooded areas
Similarity to toxic species: Poison hemlock
Best time: Early spring or fall
Status: Widespread
Tools needed: Trowel

A view of the plant.
KEIR MORSE

Properties

Different species can have a slender to stout appearance, arising from a thickly clustered perennial root. It can grow up to 4 feet tall, though it's usually not quite that tall. The stems are hollow, as are the stems of poison hemlock, so make certain you've identified this before you eat it. Perhaps the best way to differentiate this plant from poison hemlock (and other members of this group) is the obvious licorice aroma. Leaves are two to three pinnately divided, with three to five leaflets, with each leaflet being lanceolate to rounded, and either serrate or pinnately divided. Flowers are arranged in loose, compound umbels. Petals can be white, purple, yellow, or pink, with narrowed tips. The different species can be definitively determined by the shape of the seeds, which could be long and tapered, or not, and in other configurations. The seeds of *O. occidentalis* are about 12 to 22 millimeters long. These small fruits point upward, and are nearly black when dried. The flowers of *O. occidentalis* are yellow.

Uses

The plant is used as a seasoning for other foods because of the strong anise (or licorice) aroma. Though you could use it alone, it's best as an additive to other dishes, or to flavor various teas and beverages. Native Americans of the area typically used this plant, both leaves and roots, to season other foods.

The root is often used, alone or with other substances, to improve digestion. Studies have indicated that this root, specifically *O. occidentalis*, might be particularly good for treating candidiasis and fungal infections of the digestive tract, and of the reproductive system.

Cautions

You'd probably not confuse this plant for poison hemlock because the leaves of poison hemlock are a bit more finely divided, and the plant lacks the anise aroma. It could be possible to confuse sweet cicely with water hemlock though, again, water hemlock lacks the licorice aroma.

Always exercise caution before consuming any member of the Parsley family. Ideally, always see the plant in the wild with a plant authority or expert before you consume any wild plants.

YAMPA
Perideridia gairdneri, formerly *P. montana*

There are about a dozen species of *Perideridia* worldwide, and at least four of them are found in Idaho.

Use: All parts of the plant are edible, though the roots are most commonly eaten.
Range: Most often in grassy meadows
Similarity to toxic species: See Cautions.
Best time: For a more tender root, dig it in the spring. Seeds can be gathered in autumn.
Status: Widespread; can be found up into Canada, east beyond Idaho, and south to Colorado
Tools needed: Trowel

Properties
This is a perennial, growing from 2 to 3½ feet tall. Yampa is an obvious member of the Parsley family, with its white flowers in compound umbels typically appearing in July and August. The narrow linear segments of the leaves are pin-nately divided, or ternate-pinnately compound. Leaves are from 1 to 12 inches long, which is quite a range, but it all depends on the soil conditions in which the plant is growing. Yampa appear almost grass-like, blending in well with grasses so they are hardly noticed until they flower. The root is small, somewhat rounded at one end, and comes to a point at the other end. Often the roots are formed in pairs.

Uses
When the leaves are tender, they can be added to salads and used as a nibble. The flowers can likewise be used in salads, or cooked.

The flowering yampa plant. MARGO BORS

However, the small roots are the most desirable part of this plant, tasty both raw and cooked. The raw roots have a nutty flavor, like a water chestnut, and also reminiscent of a spicy carrot. These can be chopped into salads, or just used as a snack. They are mild and tasty when baked or boiled, and you'll find that no one rejects this pleasant food. Their small size, however, means you'll be putting in your work to get enough for a meal. Tom Elpel, in his *Foraging the Mountain West* books, says it takes him about an hour with a digging stick to harvest just a cup of the roots.

Cautions

Because the deadly poison hemlock is in this family, and therefore has the same floral structure, you must be absolutely certain you are identifying yampa if you intend to eat it. There are several significant differences between yampa and poison hemlock. Poison hemlock can grow to 7 feet tall, with stout hollow stems blotched with purple as the plant matures. An observant forager should not confuse poison hemlock for yampa.

Also, be a conscientious forager. Loosen the soil so you can remove the largest roots, but then return the smaller ones back to the soil for the following years.

A view of the yampa flower. TOM ELPEL

A view of the yampa root. TOM ELPEL

Lewis and Clark

On August 26, 1805, Lewis wrote the following description of yampa, which he observed in Idaho and called "fennel." "I observe the Indian women collecting the root of a speceis of fennel which grows in the moist grounds and feeding their poor starved children . . . The radix [root] of this plant is of the knob kind, of a long ovate form terminating in a single radicle [root], the whole bing about 3 or four inches in length and the thickest part about the size of a man's little finger. It is white firm and crisp in it's present state, when dryed and pounded it makes a fine white meal; the flavor of this root is not unlike that of annis-seed but not so pungent; the stem rises to the hight of 3 or 4 feet is jointed smooth and cilindric; from 1 to 4 of those knobed roots are attached to the base of this stem. The leaf is sheathing sessile [no stalk to the leaf] . . . the divisions long and narrow; the whole is of a deep green. It is now in blume; the flowers are numerous, small, petals white, and are arranged in the umbellaferous kind . . ." On May 18, 1806, Lewis describes how he observes Sacagawea collecting a store of yampa roots for the travel in the Rocky Mountains. Lewis states that the Shoshone call the root the "year-pah."

DOGBANE FAMILY (APOCYNACEAE)

The Dogbane family has 200 to 450 genera, and between 3,000 and 5,000 species worldwide.

MILKWEED
Asclepias speciosa

A view of the unique milkweed flowers. Note the fuzzy leaves. LILY JANE TSONG

The genus *Asclepias* contains about one hundred members, with about eight found in Idaho.

Use: Young shoots, leaves, pods are boiled and eaten.

Range: Widespread in both disturbed soils and some wilderness areas

Similarity to toxic species: Could bear a resemblance to some dogbanes

Best time: Collect the shoots early, and the leaves before the plant flowers. The pods are available in early summer.

Status: Common

Tools needed: A bag, clippers

Milkweed with flower buds.

Properties

Milkweed is found throughout the United States. This plant grows erect, from 2 to 5 feet tall, is stout, and is whitish-green in color. It is usually found in patches. The stalk is fibrous and usually erect. Thick milky-white sap oozes out when the stalk or leaf is broken or cut. The ovate-to-oblong leaves are opposite or whorled, not toothed at the margins, and tapered at both ends, measuring up to 5 inches long. The white, pink, or rose/purplish flowers are about ½ inch in diameter, arranged in umbels. Each flower consists of a five-petaled corolla; each petal has an erect cowl and inwardly hooked horn. There are five sepals, five stamens, and two pistils with a superior ovary. The blossoms develop into rough green pods (fruits) about 3 inches long. When the pods mature, they split along one seam, revealing the neatly packed seeds. A number of down-like silky fibers are attached to each seed.

Uses

The tender young sprouts, below 6 inches tall, can be eaten. When the plant is older, the leaves and flower clusters are also used for food. The immature seedpods—before they've developed the silky fibers inside (cut one open and inspect)—are great in soup or with meat. All parts of the milkweed must be boiled in water before they are rendered palatable. I used to follow Euell Gibbons's warnings to always double and even triple boil milkweed before eating because it was said to be so bitter. However, just taste it before eating. Sometimes one boiling will do the job.

A patch of milkweed.

A view of the flowers and mature pods of milkweed.

Cautions

According to Dr. James Adams, "Milkweed contains glycosides that can be bad for the human heart in high doses. Be careful to use the young shoots and boil them." Ingestion of raw milkweed can cause severe stomach and intestinal upsets. Symptoms, which occur within a few hours after eating, include staggering, difficult breathing, excessive perspiration, enlarged pupils, weakness, muscle spasms, and a high temperature. *A. speciosa* has resulted in livestock poisoning, but most animals tend to avoid it. There are several species of milkweed across the country, and *A. syriaca* (common in the East) and *A. California* and *A. fascicularis* (common in the West) are the ones most commonly eaten. Nationwide, there are about sixty species, twenty-five of these occurring in the West.

PIPEVINE FAMILY (ARISTOLOCHIACEAE)

There are ten genera of this family, with about 600 species worldwide.

WILD GINGER
Asarum canadense

There are 90 species of *Asarum* worldwide, and three species in Idaho.

Use: Root or leaves used as you would use cultivated ginger, mostly as a seasoning or medicine
Range: This plant prefers moist and shady areas.
Similarity to toxic species: None
Best time: Spring to late fall
Status: Somewhat common
Tools needed: Trowel

Properties

The entire plant is no more than about 10 inches tall.

This is a perennial, with leaves arising from a branching horizontal rhizome. The pair of leaves have long stems that arise directly from the root. The leaves

Wild ginger. KEIR MORSE.

are more or less heart-shaped, or arrowhead-shaped, and are sometimes mottled. The leaf and leaf stalks are covered in fine hairs.

The plants are often somewhat conspicuous because of the pair of heart-shaped leaves. Sometimes they are solitary, and you might also find them in patches. At times, they are hidden by the leaves of the forest floor. These leaves are aromatic.

The flowers are solitary on each leafless stalk. The flowers, which appear in late spring, are brownish-purple with three sepals and no petals, twelve stamens, and one pistil.

Wild ginger. KEIR MORSE.

Uses

This is used as you would use commercial ginger root, as a candy, seasoning, or medicinal plant. If you've used ginger for cooking, you'll have no trouble working with this root.

The root is easily dug, and can be used fresh, or dried for later use. If you want to make a ginger candy, slice the root into small slices and boil in water until tender. To make the candy, follow any candy recipe from a good cookbook.

The root can also be simply soaked in any sweetened water. You can then use the water for cooking, or for drinking as is.

You also can slice the slender roots into thin segments and use in Chinese recipes, either fresh or dried. The dried root can also be ground finely, and added to salad dressings or pickling spices.

If made into a candy or infusion, wild ginger is said to be effective in soothing sore throats as well as for relieving stomach pains and intestinal disorders.

Yes, we admit this is a marginal food, though it often catches the eye because of the heart-shaped appearance of the leaves.

Cautions

Consume wild ginger sparingly. The plant contains aristolochic acid, which can damage the kidneys. This acid is not readily water-soluble, so confections made from steeping the plant in water may be more benign. Aristolochic acid is present in plants of the Aristolochia and Asarum genera. In 2001, the FDA issued a warning about kidney damage and possible urinary tract cancer in people who consume them, so it is important to use small amounts of these plants.

SUNFLOWER FAMILY (ASTERACEAE)

Worldwide, the Sunflower family has about 1,500 genera and about 23,000 species! This is the largest family in Idaho, with 142 genera.

Willis Linn Jepson, author of *The Jepson Manual: Higher Plants of California*, divides this very large family into fourteen groups. Most of the plants addressed here are in Group 7, described as having ligulate heads, five-lobed ligules (five teeth per petal), and generally containing milky sap when broken. When I was studying botany in the 1970s, my teachers described this group as "the Chicory Tribe," a much more descriptive title than the unimaginative "Group 7."

According to Dr. Leonid Enari, the Chicory Tribe contains no poisonous members and is a worthy group for further edibility research. I have eaten many members of this group not listed here, though generally they require extensive boiling and water changing to render them edible and palatable.

GROUP 4

BURDOCK
Arctium minus

There are ten species of *Arctium* throughout Europe, and only *A. minus* has been recorded in Idaho.

Use: Root, stems, and leaves can be eaten.
Range: Not a native, but can be found throughout the state. Prefers old orchards, waste areas, and fields.
Similarity to toxic species: Resembles a rhubarb leaf
Best time: Best time to dig the root is in the first year's growth.
Status: Relatively common
Tools needed: Shovel

Properties

Wild burdock is found throughout Idaho, and throughout most of the United States. The first time I saw wild burdock, I thought I was looking at a rhubarb plant, though the stalk was not red and celery-like, as with rhubarb.

The first-year plant produces a rosette of rhubarb-type leaves; in ideal soil, the second-year plant produces a stalk 6 to 9 feet tall.

The leaves are heart-shaped (cordate) or broadly ovate. The leaves are conspicuously veined. The first-year leaves are large and up to 2 feet in length. In the second season, the plant sends up a flower stalk with similar, but smaller, leaves. The purple to white flowers, compressed in bur-like heads, bloom in July and August. The seed containers are spiny-hooked burs that stick to socks and pants.

A Burdock leaf.

Burdock seeds. JEAN PAWEK

The cut burdock root.

Burdock's root looks like an elongated cultivated carrot, except that the wild burdock is white inside with a brownish-gray skin that is peeled away before eating. You sometimes find this root in the markets sold as "gobo."

Uses

The first-year roots can be dug, washed, and eaten once peeled. They are usually simmered in water until tender and cooked with other vegetables. In Russia, the roots have been used as potato substitutes when potatoes aren't available. Roots can be peeled and sliced into thin pieces and sautéed or cooked with vegetables. I also eat young tender roots diced into salad, and I find them very tasty.

Leaves can be eaten once boiled; in some cases, two boilings are necessary, depending on your taste. Try to get them very young. Peeled leaf stems can be eaten raw or cooked. The erect flower stalks, collected before the flowers open, can be peeled of their bitter green skin and then dried or cooked, though these tend to be much more fibrous than the leaf stems.

An analysis of the root (100 grams or ½ cup) shows 50 milligrams (mg) of calcium, 58 mg of phosphorus, and 180 mg of potassium. Tea of the roots is said to be useful in treating rheumatism.

Herbalists all over the world use burdock: The roots and seeds are a soothing demulcent, tonic, and alterative (restorative to normal health).

A view of the burdock leaf, first year. LOUIS-M. LANDRY

According to Linda Sheer, who grew up in rural Kentucky, burdock leaf was the best herbal treatment her people used for rattlesnake bites. Two leaves are simmered in milk and given to the victim to drink. The burdock helps to counteract the effects of the venom. The body experiences both shock and calcium loss as a result of a rattlesnake bite. The lactose in the milk offsets the calcium loss and prevents or reduces shock. (I'd love to hear from chemists about how specifically burdock helps a rattlesnake victim recover.)

You can also take the large burdock leaves and wrap fish and game in them before roasting in the coals of a fire pit. Foods cooked this way are mildly seasoned by the leaves.

THISTLE
Cirsium spp.

Worldwide, there are about 200 species in the *Cirsium* genus. At least nineteen are found in Idaho, not including varieties.

Use: Edible stems, youngest leaves
Range: Found throughout the United States, and widely in Idaho
Similarity to toxic species: None
Best time: Spring
Status: Widespread
Tools needed: Knife, clippers, bag

Properties
There are many species of thistle, all with very similar appearances. Thistle normally reaches 4 to 5 feet at maturity. They can be either perennial or biennial herbs.

Thistle leaves are alternate, prickly or spiny, and generally toothed. They're about 8 inches long at maturity. Thistle flowers are clustered in bristly heads. They are crimson, purple, pink, and occasionally white. The lower half of the flower heads are covered with spiny bracts, resembling thistle's cultivated relative, the artichoke.

Uses
When the plant is young and no flower stalk has emerged, the root can be dug, boiled, and eaten. These are starchy, mild-flavored roots. As the plant flowers, the root becomes tough and fibrous. If you want to try eating the roots, search in the spring in rich soil. If the soil and the timing are not right, the root is too tough to eat.

My favorite part of the thistle is the stalk cut before the flowers develop while it is still tender and perhaps about 3 feet tall. Using a sharp knife, I first cut off the bristly leaves, and then carefully scrape off the spiny outer layer so I can handle it. Once the stalk is scraped of its outer fibrous layer, you can eat it raw—it is

The thistle flower. RICK ADAMS

Kai examines the ladybugs and aphids on this thistle plant. Thistle stems are best eaten when very young—and wash off the bugs first! LILY JANE TSONG

sweet and somewhat reminiscent of celery. We've served it with peanut butter for a tasty snack.

These cleaned stalks can be baked, boiled, sautéed, or added to other foods. They can be served with butter or cheese, as you might serve asparagus.

If you've ever seen a garden artichoke, then the relationship of artichoke to thistle might be obvious. Can you eat the flowering head of the thistle like you'd eat an artichoke? Well, it depends. First, you have to clip the thistle flower while it's still young, and before it has actually flowered. You boil it, and then if you peel back all the scaly bracts, you'll find just a little bit of the tender heart there. It's very tasty, and worth trying, but usually there is really not enough heart in the wild thistle to make it worth your bother.

In general, I don't eat the leaves because I find the prickliness irritating. However, if you can find the very youngest growth of spring, you can collect some very tasty greens that would even be good in a salad. On occasion, when the timing was right, I was able to collect many of the very young, emerging cotyledons and add them to salads and cooked dishes. Since the flavor of the leaves is a bit sweet, you could collect young leaves and process them in a juicer that removes the pulp and have a tasty and healthy drink.

GROUP 5

PINEAPPLE WEED
Matricaria discoidea, formerly *M. matricarioides*

There are seven species of *Matricaria* worldwide, with two found in Idaho.

Use: The entire plant can be used for a pleasant tea.
Range: Widespread, preferring hard soils
Similarity to toxic species: Superficially resembles very young poison hemlock
Best time: Spring, when the flowers are present
Status: Prefers hard-packed soils
Tools needed: Sharp knife or scissors, bag

Properties
This is a relative of the chamomile plant, so if you've ever grown chamomile, you have a good idea of the general appearance of pineapple weed. You most commonly find the plant growing in rock-hard soil, maybe where cars have driven—the type of soil where you cannot easily stick in a shovel.

This is an annual herb that can rise as much as 8 inches, but is usually less tall than that—typically 3 or 4 inches. The leaves are finely divided into short, narrow linear segments, which are alternately arranged and glabrous (not hairy). The flower heads are formed at the ends or tips of the branches and are cone-shaped and small, about ½ inch in length. There are no ray flowers on the pineapple weed, meaning no petals.

When you crush the leaves, and particularly the greenish flower head, you get a distinctive aroma of pineapple, hence the name. Some will find the aroma suggestive of common chamomile.

Sometimes pineapple weed will grow in thick patches, getting a few inches tall.

A view of the pineapple weed. LILY JANE TSONG

A close-up of the pineapple weed plant.

Uses

I have had the young heads served as a garnish in salads, and even tossed into soups. But most of the time, the plant is used to make a pleasant beverage. Pineapple weed is closely related to chamomile, and, according to Dr. Enari, its active chemistry is a bit weaker than chamomile. Nevertheless, it is used medicinally in all the ways you'd use chamomile, such as for its calming effect. Additionally, many people commonly use it as a beverage simply because they enjoy its flavor.

The whole aboveground herb can be cut and infused to make a pleasant tea. Or, you can snip off just the flowers to make an even more flavorful beverage. Some people find the flavor of the entire herb a bit bitter, and so we can say this is an acquired taste. If you want to take the time, you can just pick the flowers and brew them, and this doesn't carry the bitterness that you'll find with the leaf.

You can dry this herb for later, out-of-season use, or you can use it fresh when it's in season. Drink plain or sweetened, as you wish.

Cautions

Since these low-growing plants are so close to the ground, be sure to wash them well before using.

Views of the low-growing pineapple weed.

GROUP 7 (or 8, depending on which botanist you follow): heads ligulate; ligules five-lobed, generally white sap present

CHICORY
Cichorium intybus

There are about six species of *Cichorium* worldwide; only this one is found in Idaho. You can occasionally find the related endive, which is not common, near gardens or farms where the endive has a chance to go feral.

Use: Root for beverage and food; greens raw or cooked
Range: Widespread throughout the United States; found especially in the disturbed soils of farms, fields, and gardens
Similarity to toxic species: None Best time: Spring
Status: Common
Tools needed: Digging tool for roots

Properties
The chicory plant grows upright, typically 3 to 5 feet tall, with prominent sky-blue flowers. Look carefully at the flower—each petal is divided into five teeth, typical of the Chicory Tribe of the Sunflower family. Each leaf will produce a bit

Flowers of chicory. RICK ADAMS

Chicory flower.
VICKIE SHUFER

of milky sap when cut. The older upper leaves on the stalk very characteristically clasp the stem at the base.

This is a perennial from Europe that is now widespread in parts of Idaho, mostly in fields, gardens, disturbed soils, and along roadsides.

Uses

This is another of those incredibly nutritious plants with multiple uses. The leaves can be added to salads, preferably the very young leaves. If you don't mind a bit of bitterness, the older leaves can be added to salads too. The leaves can be cooked like spinach and added to a variety of dishes, such as soups, stews, and egg dishes.

Chicory roots are also used, either boiled and buttered or sliced and added to stews and soups. Roots in rich soil tend to be less woody and fibrous.

Chicory roots have long been used as a substitute for coffee or as a coffee extender. Dig and wash the roots, and then dry them, grind them, and then roast them until they are brown. Use as you would regular coffee grounds, alone or as a coffee extender. Incidentally, you can make this same coffee substitute/extender with the roots of dandelion and sow thistle.

Note: The entire Chicory Tribe of the Sunflower family contains no poisonous members, though many are bitter. These are generally tender-leafed plants with milky sap and "dandelion-like" flowers, each petal of which usually has five teeth at the tip.

PRICKLY LETTUCE
Lactuca serriola, et al.

There are about one hundred species of *Lactuca* worldwide, with at least five found in Idaho. *Lactuca serriola*, a European native, is probably the most abundant and widespread.

Use: Young leaves, raw or cooked
Range: Found throughout the United States, most commonly in gardens, disturbed soils, along trails, and at the edges of farms
Similarity to toxic species: None
Best time: Early spring
Status: Widespread

Properties
Prickly lettuce is a very common annual plant that you can find just about anywhere, hidden in plain view. Yes, you've seen it, but it likely blended into the landscape. It's mostly an "urban weed," though occasionally you'll find it in the "near wilderness" surrounding urban areas.

Young rosette of prickly lettuce, still OK in salads.

The stalk of the maturing prickly lettuce plant.

Prickly lettuce rises with its erect stalk to generally no more than 3 feet. The young leaves are lanceolate with generally rounded ends. They are tender, and if you tear a leaf, you'll see white sap. The plant grows upright with an erect stem, which develops soft spines as it gets older. As the plant matures, you'll note that there is a stiff line of hairs on the bottom midrib of the leaf. The leaf attachment is either sessile or clasping the stem, and the leaf shape can be quite variable, from a simple oblong-lanceolate leaf to one that is divided into pinnately lobed segments. After you've seen a few prickly lettuce plants, you should readily recognize them.

The flowers are small and dandelion-like, pale yellow, with about a dozen ray flowers per head. As with dandelion, these mature into small seeds attached to a little cottony tuft.

Uses

Prickly lettuce sounds like something you'd really like in a salad, but, in fact, you need to find the very youngest leaves or they get too tough and bitter. Very young leaves (before the plant has sent up its flower stalk) are good added to your salads and sandwiches. The

Here's why you don't eat the mature prickly lettuce leaves!

leaves can also be collected and mixed into stir-fries, or added to soups or any sort of stew to which you would add wild greens.

But let's not be fooled by the name "lettuce." Yes, it's botanically a relative of the cultivar you buy in the supermarket, but the leaves become significantly bitter as they age, and the rib on the underside of each older leaf develops stiff spines that makes any similarity to lettuce very distant. This means you'll be using this plant raw only when it's very young, and when it's flowering and mature, you probably won't be using it at all.

Still, it's edible, and it grows everywhere. You should get to know this plant, and its relatives, and learn to recognize it early in the growing season.

I've used it when very young in sandwiches, salads, soups, stews, and egg dishes. I even used the small root when I was experimenting with coffee substitutes. Since prickly lettuce is related to dandelion and sow thistle, I figured it would work well as a coffee substitute, and it does, but there's very little root to this plant.

FORAGER NOTE: One of the common names for this plant is "compass plant." When the plant is mature, the edges of the leaves tend to point to the sun as the sun moves across the sky. This is probably a mechanism to stop water loss. While this is by no means as accurate as using a compass, it could help you determine directions with a bit of figuring.

SOW THISTLE
Sonchus oleraceus, et al.

There are about fifty-five species of *Sonchus* worldwide. Three are found in Idaho, all of which are from Europe and are edible.

Use: Mostly the leaves, raw or cooked; root can be cooked and eaten; flower buds pickled
Range: Found throughout the United States; most common in urban areas, gardens, and on farms, but can be found in most environments
Similarity to toxic species: None
Best time: Spring, though the older leaves of late summer are still useful
Status: Common
Tools needed: Trowel for digging

Properties
Though the common sow thistle (*S. oleraceus*) is most commonly used for food, the other three species found in Idaho look very similar and can be used the same way. When you see *S. asper*, the prickly sow thistle, you may conclude that it's too much work to use for a dish of cooked greens because it is covered with soft spines.

When most people see a flowering common sow thistle for the first time, they think it's a dandelion. Yes, it is related to the dandelion, and, yes, the flowers are very similar.

Here is a simple distinction: All dandelion leaves arise directly from the taproot, forming a basal rosette. Sow thistle sends up a much taller stalk—up to 5 feet or so in ideal conditions, but usually about 3 feet. The leaves are formed along this more or less erect and branching stalk. The leaves are paler and more tender than dandelion leaves, and sow thistle leaves are not as jagged on the edges as dandelion. Though the individual dandelion and sow thistle flowers are very similar, dandelion only forms one flower per stalk, whereas sow thistle will form many flowers per stalk.

Uses
Though sow thistle may not be quite as nutritious as dandelion, it's definitely tastier and the leaves are more tender. You can include the leaves of sow thistle in salads, and even when the plant is old, there is only a hint of bitterness. The flavor and texture are very much like lettuce you might grow in your garden.

The leaves and tender stems are also ideally added to soups and stews, or simply cooked up by themselves and served like spinach greens. They are tasty alone, or you can try adding different seasonings (peppers, butter, cheese) that you enjoy.

A view of the sow thistle plant.

FORAGER NOTE: Sow thistle is one of our most common wild foods. It is so widespread that it can be found in nearly every environment, even in the cracks of urban sidewalks.

A bee collecting sow thistle nectar.

The root can be eaten or made into a coffee substitute, as is commonly done with two of its relatives, dandelion and chicory. To eat the roots, gather the young ones and boil till tender. Season as you wish, and serve. The roots could also be washed and added to soups and stews.

For a coffee substitute, gather and wash the roots, then dry thoroughly. Grind them into a coarse meal, roast to a light shade of brown, and then percolate into a caffeine-free beverage. Is it "good"? It's all a matter of personal preference.

RECIPE

Spring Awakening

For a dish that resembles asparagus, use just the tender sow thistle stems in the springtime (the leaves can be removed and added to other dishes). Boil or steam the stems until tender—it doesn't take long—and then lay them on your plate like asparagus. Add some cheese or butter, and these will make a delicious dish, but one you'll only enjoy in the spring. Timing is everything.

DANDELION
Taraxacum officinale

There are about sixty species of *Taraxacum* worldwide, with at least four of these found in Idaho.

Use: Leaves raw or cooked; root cooked or processed into a beverage
Range: Common nationwide; prefers lawns, fields, and disturbed soils
Similarity to toxic species: None
Best time: Spring for the greens; anytime for the roots
Status: Common
Tools needed: Trowel for the roots

Properties
Even people who say they don't know how to identify any plants can probably identify a dandelion in a field. The characteristic yellow composite flower sits atop the narrow stem, which arises directly from the taproot. There is one yellow flower per flower stalk. These mature into the round, puffy seed heads that children like to blow on and make a wish.

Dandelions grow in fields, lawns, vacant lots, and along trails. They tend to prefer disturbed soils, though I have seen them in the wilderness.

The leaves are dark green, toothed on the margins, and each arises from the root. The name "dandelion" actually comes from the French *dent de leon*, meaning "tooth of the lion," for the jagged edges of the leaves.

Dandelion in flower.

Dandelion rosette and seeding flowerheads.

Uses

My first exposure to dandelion was at about age seven, when my father would pay me a nickel to dig them out of our front yard lawn and throw them into the trash. Boy, things have changed! These days, I would not consider having a front lawn, and I definitely would not dig out the dandelions and toss them in the trash.

Dandelion is another versatile wild food. It's not native to Idaho, but is now found all over the world. The yellow flowers make the plant conspicuous in fields and lawns, though it's really the leaves and root that are most used by the forager.

If you want raw dandelion greens, you'll want to pick them as early as possible in the spring season, or they become bitter. The bitterness is not bad, and it can be mellowed out by adding other greens. Also, an oil-rich dressing makes a dandelion salad more palatable.

Dandelion rosette.

A cup of dandelion greens contains over 100 percent of the recommended daily allowance (RDA) for vitamin A, which (among other things) is good for the skin. A cup also contains over 500 percent of the RDA for vitamin K. It's a great source of many vitamins and minerals, including the B vitamins and lutein. This has led some to call it "poor man's ginseng."

It's understandable that dandelions have gotten more popular—they are, after all, the richest source of beta-carotene, even richer than carrots. However, not all the greens sold as "dandelion" in farmers' markets and supermarkets are the genuine leaf. Frequently we will see various endive relatives sold and called "dandelion."

The roots are also edible. The younger roots, and roots of plants growing in rich soil, are more tender and more desirable. But I have eaten old roots and tough roots, and have found a way to make them palatable. Generally, I scrub the roots to get rid of all the soil, and then boil until tender. You can boil them whole or slice them, and when tender, use them in stews and soups.

For a "coffee-substitute" beverage, wash and then dry the roots. Though there are a few ways you can do this, I generally do a coarse grind, and then roast in the oven until the grounds are mildly brown. Then I do a fine grind, and percolate them into a beverage. You can drink it "black" or add honey and cream.

SALSIFY
Tragopogon spp.

There are about forty-five species of *Tragopogon* worldwide, and five have been identified in Idaho, having either yellow or purple flowers. All are introduced.

Use: The root is used most commonly; the tender leaves can also be eaten.
Range: Widespread in lower elevations, along roadsides, hillsides, and in developed areas
Similarity to toxic species: None
Best time: Roots are best gathered in the spring; greens can be collected anytime, but are best in the spring.
Status: Relatively common
Tools needed: Shovel

Properties

Salsify is a fairly widespread and easy-to-recognize plant. Most folks initially notice the large dandelion-like flower, except it is on a much taller stalk, perhaps 2 feet tall. Depending on the species, the flower may be yellow or purple, and it will have noticeable bracts that extend beyond the petals. The yellow flower is typically *T. dubius*. The purple flower is *T. porrifolius*.

The seed head is just like the dandelion seed head, but bigger and very round, around 4 inches in diameter. The leaves are linear, almost grass-like, and will exude a milky sap when broken (like dandelion or sow thistle).

Salsify is a biennial plant, meaning that it produces leaves in the first year, and in the second year it sends up its flower stalk before it dies. The roots of the first-year plant are the most tender. If you pick the root from a flowering plant, it will be tough and a bit bitter. These are sometimes cultivated, and in those cases, are likely to produce larger and more tender roots. But in the wild, the roots you're likely to find are thin, like pencils.

A close-up of the salsify flower.
RICK ADAMS

Uses

Salsify, also called oyster plant, is most often used for the root. Before I ever ate one, I read the descriptions of "large fleshy roots" with an oyster flavor, and imagined something like a carrot or radish that would cook up into some exotic seafood-like dish. However, the reality is a little different. Most of the time I find the plant growing in compacted and hard soil, where the root has never had a chance to get large and fleshy. It is more like a slender carrot, a bit fibrous, and though the flavor is somewhat bland, the texture is improved by cooking.

Of course, it didn't help that when I was first digging up salsify roots, they were all from the flowering plants, because those were the only ones I was able to

The salsify plant. RICK ADAMS

A round seeding head of salsify. RICK ADAMS

recognize as salsify. But these were the older, second-year plants with tougher roots.

Yes, there are cases where you will find an easy-to-dig root that is pretty darn good, such as during the rainy season in mulchy soil. Either way, this is such a common plant that you should at least try it. And because it's an introduced exotic, no one will mind if you do some volunteer weed removal.

Try cooking it to tenderize, and then slice the root and add to soups and stews. In general, you'll need to

A view of the seeding flower head. LILY JANE TSONG

cook these roots about two to three times as long as you'd need to cook potatoes. Does it really taste like oyster? Maybe; maybe not. Perhaps there is a slight flavor reminiscent of something like oyster.

We have also cooked up all of the aboveground plant, and eaten all that was tender. The stalk will usually be tough, but the leaves are tasty and chewy.

William Schlegel reports that his favorite parts of salsify are the flower buds of *Tragopogon dubius*. He uses them as a nibble when he's out on his land. At the bud stage, these are tender and make a mild vegetable.

When doing underground pit cooking, we have covered potatoes and onions and meat with the upper part of the salsify plant, which was abundant. Not only did these leaves protect the vegetables we were steaming, but we found these greens to be a tasty addition to our meal as well.

Lore

Sometimes, salsify is known as "John goes to bed at noon." The flowers begin to slowly close around 11 a.m., and are closed by noon. The flowers stay closed for two to three hours, and then open around 3 p.m., and then stay open until dark when they close again. These plants were sometimes used in European "clock gardens."

GROUP 9

ARROWLEAF BALSAMROOT
Balsamorhiza sagittata

There are ten recorded species of *Balsamorhiza*, all of which have been recorded in Idaho. *B. sagittata* seems to have been used the most, along with *B. deltoidea*.

Use: All parts can be used for food, though the root is most desirable.
Range: Widespread throughout the southern part of Idaho
Similarity to toxic species: None
Best time: Roots are best gathered in the spring; greens can be collected anytime, but are best in the spring.
Status: Relatively common
Tools needed: Digging bar or small trowel

Properties
This somewhat conspicuous perennial has large, arrowhead-shaped leaves. The leaves are covered with soft hairs, giving them a pale green to whitish cast. The typical sunflower family flowers are typical solitary on the long (about a foot and a half) leafless stalk. Each petal is yellow. The taproot is shaped somewhat like a carrot.

Uses
The young flower and leaf stems, when only a few inches tall, can be peeled and eaten raw (see photo). The leaves and outer skin have a bitter flavor. The best leaves are collected from the young plants. The leaves and stems can be eaten raw,

A field of the flowering plant. KYLE CHAMBERLAIN

A view of Arrowleaf Balsamroot. BARRY BRECKLING

or cooked into stews, soups, or mixed greens. Cooking mellows both the flavor and texture.

Of the foragers I spoke to, a few said they enjoyed the leaves and stems, mostly cooked. A few others said that the plant is "barely palatable." The leaf

A section of the root. KYLE CHAMBERLAIN

and flower stems are best if used only in the early spring; if collected too late, they become tough, bitter, and aromatic, and you'd not likely include them in any dish.

The roots have been an important standby food. The roots are starchy and have a pleasant flavor but can be very fibrous. Young roots, carrot-size and smaller, should be collected when they are most tender, in the early spring. The roots can be steamed, boiled, or roasted, but this may not make them more tender. You may still find yourself chewing for a long time, or having to spit out fibers. This is a good example of the roughage absent from the contemporary diet.

The roots were of great importance to the Northwest tribes, who often used them in great numbers. They can be eaten raw, but they become especially flavorful when baked or boiled.

William Schlegel reports that a man from Helena, Montana, spoke before his chapter of the Montana Native Plant Society. "The man tried roasting a root and found it 'balsamiferous.' The root may not therefore be a palatable food to the modern palate or it may require specialized knowledge. I think the seeds would be a good food. Ethnobotanist Arlene BigCrane used to eat the young flower stalks with her children as a fresh green vegetable when she worked at the same elementary school as my mother . . ."

Lewis and Clark
Clark collected a specimen on April 14, 1806, above the mouth of the White Salmon River, which he called "Canoe Creek." Frederick Pursh recorded that "[t]he stem is eaten by the natives, without any preparation." Clark wrote on the same day, "After dinner we proceeded on our voyage. I walked on Shore with Shabono on the N. Side through a handsome bottom. Met several parties of women and boys in Serch of herbs & roots to Subsist on maney of them had parcels of the Stems of the Sun flower . . .", referring to the arrowleaf balsamroot.

COMMON SUNFLOWER
Helianthus annus

There are sixty-seven known species of *Helianthus*, with at least six recorded in Idaho, not counting subspecies.

Use: Mostly seed for food
Range: Plains, prairies, roadsides, fields
Similarity to toxic species: None
Best time: Seeds are best collected when the plant matures in summer.
Status: Widespread
Tools needed: A collection bag

Properties

You've no doubt seen flowers in fields many times and thought, "Hey, there's a sunflower." Maybe it was, maybe it wasn't. After all, the Sunflower family is one of the largest botanical families. If what you saw was tall, and looked very much like the sunflower plants that we grow in our gardens, but perhaps just a bit smaller, then you've likely encountered the actual sunflower plant.

The wild sunflower thrives in this front yard. LILY JANE TSONG

The sunflower plant can grow up to 8 feet tall, with its erect stem usually unbranched, but sometimes branched. It's covered in stiff hairs. The leaves are alternately arranged, and are generally triangular in shape; they are more or less heart-shaped and narrow to a tip. The leaves are also covered in stiff hairs.

It's the flower that is universally recognized. The flower heads are around 6 inches across, with yellow ray flowers ("petals"). The flowers of the central disk have no showy petals, and are brown. The fruits are single-seeded, dry, and flat.

Sunflowers are common in disturbed soils, roadsides, plains, prairies, and fields.

Uses

The seeds are the primary food, though sometimes the wild sunflowers do not produce the abundant volumes of seed to make gathering worthwhile, or the seeds can be very small and dry. If there is a sufficient volume for collecting, they are collected when ripe, and shelled. The seeds are then used in bread products and pastries, desserts, drinks, and as snacks. The shelled seeds can be used raw or roasted, in any recipes calling for nuts, including breads and cakes. Finely ground sunflower seeds (shell and all when they are tiny) can be used as a partial substitute for flour in some recipes.

Native people would roast and grind the entire seed into a fine flour. The flour would then be mixed with water and made into a drink, or made into a dough and mixed with other ingredients.

William Schlegel told me about the classic book *Buffalo Bird Woman's Garden*, where the author talks about how hard it is to grind sunflower seeds, and so

A single sunflower. BARBARA EISENSTEIN

she grinds them shell and all. Schlegel pointed out that sunflower seeds can be hard to shell even with modern equipment. "Imagine the fiber!" said Schlegel.

One method to separate shell from seed is to coarsely break the seeds and pour them all into water. The seeds will sink and the shells will float, and can be removed. The shells have been dried and roasted and used to make a coffee-substitute, often mixed with other ingredients.

The wild sunflower seed doesn't make as good a nut butter as the cultivated sunflower seed. However, you can still grind the shelled seeds, and mix with honey, butter, or various oils to make a wild sunflower butter.

Tales from Appalachia

Linda Sheer from rural Kentucky was a friend and mentor. She told me that when her people didn't have enough "regular" food, the young immature flower heads of the sunflower would be collected, boiled until tender, and eaten. She prepared and served these to us at one of our cooking classes. Though still a bit chewy and tough, they were certainly edible and palatable, and her unique seasonings made them tasty.

A view of one flower and immature buds.
BARBARA EISENSTEIN

BARBERRY FAMILY (BERBERIDACEAE)

The Barberry family consists of about sixteen genera and approximately 670 species worldwide. Only *Berberis* is found in Idaho.

OREGON GRAPE (BARBERRY)
Berberis aquifolium (formerly *Mahonia aquifolium*), and other species

The fruits of all members of the *Berberis* genus are edible. There are approximately 600 species of *Berberis* worldwide, which are widespread in North America. In Idaho, you'll find common Oregon grape (*B. aquifolium*); mountain Oregon grape (*B. nervosa*), which is not so common; and the more common *B. repens*. *B. thunbergii* and *B. vulgaris* have also been recorded.

Use: Fruits eaten raw or made into wine, jams, or jellies
Range: Found widely throughout the state; common in the mountainous and forested areas; often used as an ornamental
Similarity to toxic species: None
Best time: Summer
Status: Common
Tools needed: Berry-collecting basket

A view of the overall Oregon grape plant, with leaf and fruit.

Oregon grape leaf and fruit.

Properties

This is a low-growing to medium-size shrub, though some are low-growing and spreading. Leaves are alternately arranged and pinnately compound. The leaflets are holly-like, with spines along their margins. Flowers are yellow and are formed in racemes. The sepals and the petals are similar, usually in five whorls. The approximately ¼-inch fruits are bluish to purple berries, and are tightly arranged in clusters that resemble tiny grapes.

Though Oregon grape can be found throughout the state, it is most common in wooded areas. It is also planted as an ornamental, so it will be found outside its native terrain.

Uses

My experience with the Oregon grape is mostly as a trail nibble, and on occasion I have had at least a handful to mash and use as a pancake topping. These small oval berries are tart and refreshing, high in vitamin C, and make a good jelly when lightly sweetened with honey.

According to Cecilia Garcia and Dr. James D. Adams Jr. in *Healing with Medicinal Plants of the West*, the fruits of all the members of the *Berberis* genus, generally all commonly called "Oregon grape," were eaten raw or cooked by most Indians wherever the plant grew. The blue to purplish fruits of *B. nervosa* were gathered by the Yana people from the foothills and dried, then ground into a flour that was used for a mush; it is likely that many other indigenous groups did the same. Many indigenous people made drinks from these fruits. They are also quite good dried and used as a snack food, or added to cookies, cakes, or other dishes as you'd add raisins.

Garcia and Adams noted that the fruit also has antihistamine activity, which may relieve indigestion. And according to Paul Campbell, author of *Earth Pigments and Paint of the California Indians*, the fruits are especially useful in making traditional blue pigment and paint.

BIRCH FAMILY (BETULACEAE)

The Birch family consists of six genera and about 155 species worldwide. Three of these genera are found in Idaho.

HAZELNUT (BEAKED HAZELNUT)
Corylus cornuta

The *Corylus* genus has about fifteen species worldwide, with only *C. cornuta* and *C. avellana* found in Idaho. *C. cornuta* is found from British Columbia to California, east to Newfoundland and Georgia, and is separated into two varieties. *C. avellana* is not common in Idaho.

Use: Edible nuts
Range: Found on the edges of forests, slopes, and in many other habitats throughout Idaho; prefers shady environments
Similarity to toxic species: None
Best time: Late summer into fall, when nuts mature
Status: Common
Tools needed: Bag or box for collecting

A view of the leaf and fruit of the hazelnut. KEIR MORSE

Properties

This large shrub, or small tree, can grow up to 25 feet tall and can easily be confused for an alder. The leaves are oval to round, alternate, with a rounded base and pointed tip. The whole leaf is about 3 inches long, with double-toothed margins. The leaves are more or less hairy (really, more like a fine fuzz) on both sides.

The nuts, which mature from September through October, are formed in pairs. A papery, bristly, outer husk covers the nut, which has a thin brittle inner shell. When you see the exposed nut, it will remind you of a commercial filbert, to which it's related. It's relatively easy to identify this tree when you find it, and easy to harvest the nuts.

The nuts ripen in the summer and autumn, and remain clinging on the trees until they are picked, or shaken free by wind or animals.

A view of the fruit. MARGO BORS

Uses

This is an excellent nut, and you'd use it in any of the ways in which you'd use a filbert: raw, roasted, slivered, etc. This means you can shell them and eat them raw in nut mixes, in salads, and even sprinkled into bread or pancake batter. Try sprinkling them on ice cream. The nuts can also be ground into a meal and used to form cakes, or added to other pastry dough.

Nuts are one of the great survival foods, since they have the oils necessary for life. They store well a long time, provide some quick energy with no cooking, and give our bodies a lot of what they need.

A view of the tree. MARGO BORS

BORAGE (WATERLEAF) FAMILY (BORAGINACEAE)

The Borage family consists of 120 genera and about 2,300 species worldwide. At least twenty-two of these genera are found in Idaho.

MOUNTAIN BLUEBELL
Mertensia ciliata

There are about fifty species worldwide, with at least thirteen recorded in Idaho.

Use: Leaves are edible.
Range: Generally found in the mountains, along stream banks
Similarity to toxic species: None
Best time: Spring
Status: Somewhat common within its range
Tools needed: Container for collecting

Properties

This plant will grow in the dry sagebrush country of Idaho, though generally it is a mountain plant, found along streams and in meadows. Its most common range is from the foothills to the subalpine zone.

Mountain bluebells, also known as streamside bluebells, begin with many stems at a woody base, growing up to 4 feet tall with large clusters of stems and many flowers. The basal leaves are elliptical in shape, with a long petiole. The

A view of mountain bluebells in flower. JEAN PAWEK

leaves that develop on the stems are smaller, still elliptical, and are nearly stemless (sessile).

The blue flowers are formed in branched, hanging clusters, with petals approximately ½-inch long, and nearly united so that the flowers appear tubular. The styles (the stalk-like part of the pistil) extend slightly beyond the petals. The overall appearance is of hanging bells, hence the name.

In general, all the species of *Mertensia* can be used for food, and all are generally called bluebells. Sometimes these are referred to as "chiming bells" to differentiate them from the many other unrelated plants that are often also called "bluebells." There are perhaps seven to nine species of *Mertensia* in this area. The tall species that grow from 1 to 4 feet and are found in moist habitats are *M. ciliata* and *M. paniculata*. Shorter species—smaller than a foot—are found in the higher and drier subalpine to alpine areas. These include *M. oblongifolia*, *M. longiflora*, *M. bella*, and *M. perplexa*.

A view of the mountain bluebell flowers.
ROBERT STEERS

Uses

The tender leaves can be used as a hiking snack. They have a slight oyster-like flavor.

In its zone, this is one of the best green plants you can find. The leaves, tender stems, and flowers can all be used raw for salad when the entire plant is still succulent, or you can just trim off the young tips and stir-fry, steam, or sauté them. You could even add some fresh leaves to a sandwich.

Older plants can get a little hairy, though this doesn't detract from palatability. Still, older leaves are best cooked.

A beautiful image of mountain bluebells.
BARBARA EISENSTEIN

Cautions

This plant is considered toxic if you consume it in "large" quantities, due to the presence of various alkaloids. We've not heard of any recorded cases of toxicity, however.

WATERLEAF

Hydrophyllum spp.: *H. alpestre*, *H. capitatum*, *H. fendleri*, and *H. occidentale* have all been recorded in Idaho.

Use: Leaves used for food. Cooked roots of *H. capitatum* and *H. fendleri* are also used for food.

Range: Moist and preferably shaded areas in the mountains

Similarity to toxic species: None

Best time: Spring

Status: widespread in west

Tools needed: A collection bag

Properties

The leaves are mostly basal, arising from the perennial rhizome no more than 15 inches or so. Most leaves of *Hydrophyllum* are alternately arranged, and are pinnately divided. Each leaflet deeply incises nearly to the midrib of the leaf, making this somewhat easy to identify. At least one species of this genus has what is described as a palmate leaf, since it consists of only 3 to 5 leaflets.

H. occidentale is a stout, tall plant, rising to about 2 feet, typically along shaded stream banks.

The densely clustered flowers (scorpoid inflorescences) can be green, white, or violet. *H. occidentale* has bluish or white flowers. The stamens of the *H. capitatum* flower extend beyond the petals, giving this flower (and all *Hydrophyllum*

Hydrophyllum occidentale. JEAN PAWEK

Flowers of H. capitatum. JOHN DOYEN

The entire waterleaf plant, H. capitatum. JEAN PAWEK

flowers) a prickly or fuzzy appearance. All *Hydrophyllum* flowers have five sepals, five petals, five stamens, and one pistil.

These plants prefer forest clearings, stony slopes, and deciduous leaf litter, where it is often moist.

Uses

The leaves are good-flavored for salad, and can be used in any cooked dish where you might use spinach or mustard greens. They are best in the spring, though they can still be cooked and eaten when collected later in the year.

The leaves of *H. capitatum* have a surface like fine flannel, so that when it rains, water droplets are held in the leaf, hence the name "waterleaf." But because of that leaf texture, some people do not enjoy the leaf raw in salad, and only cook it. And sometimes the raw leaves have a bit of bitterness. You can decide for yourself how you'd like to serve this green.

The leaves, stems, and flowers were all used by the Native Americans of the area as an early spring green.

The roots can be used for food too, but should be cooked first.

Trail Note

There is a slight astringent quality to waterleaf leaves, and so they can be crushed and applied to minor scratches and insect bites as an expedient field remedy.

MUSTARD FAMILY (BRASSICACEAE)

The Mustard family is another large family, comprising more than 330 genera worldwide and about 3,780 species. This large family is subdivided into eight groups. In Idaho, the Mustard family is represented by at least sixty-two genera. The floral characteristics that define the Mustard family are that it has four free petals, four sepals (generally white or yellow, but other colors as well), six stamens (four long, two short), one pistil, a superior ovary, and fruits are generally a capsule or silique with two valves.

Many are cultivated for foods and some for ornamentals. My mentor, Dr. Leonid Enari, stated that he was unaware of any toxic member of this entire family, though some are more palatable than others. As a result, I have experimented with many of the Mustard family species in various parts of North America. The most obvious edible members are presented here.

The typical leaf shape for this family is lyrately pinnate, meaning it has a large terminal lobe and smaller lateral lobes. Once I asked a fellow botanist for help in identifying the genus of a plant I'd found, which I knew was in the Mustard family. He replied, "Trying to identify a *Brassicacea* when not in flower is not exactly fun." Well said! These are much easier to identify once they have flowered.

MUSTARD
Brassica spp.

There are thirty-five species worldwide, and many are found throughout the United States. At least four species are found in Idaho.

Mustard leaves and stems.

A view of the mustard leaf and rosette.

Barbara Kolander collecting mustard flowers.

Use: Leaves raw or cooked; seeds for spice; flowers for garnish

Range: Fields, urban areas, lowlands, hillsides

Similarity to toxic species: None

Best time: Spring for greens and flowers

Status: Widespread

Tools needed: None

Properties

Though you should learn to recognize the common mustards even when the plant is not in flower, it is the flower that will initially draw you to the plant. The bright yellow flower has the typical Mustard family flora arrangement: four petals (shaped in an X or cross), four sepals (one under each petal), six stamens (four long, two short), and one pistil. These are formed in a raceme with the buds toward the tops, then the mature flowers, and then, lower on the stalk, the seedpods forming. The seedpods are about an inch long and needle thin.

The initial basal leaves are lyrately pinnately divided, meaning they have the appearance of a guitar with a large round lateral lobe and smaller side lobes. Not exactly like a guitar, but that gives you a good mental picture. As the plant matures, the leaves that form on the upper stalks are smaller and linear and look nothing like the young basal leaves.

Uses

Mustard is one of the first wild foods that I began to eat, partly because it is so common, and partly because it is so easy to identify. I recall seeing a line drawing

A mustard rosette.

of it in Bradford Angier's book *Free for the Eating*, which didn't look anything like the green plant with yellow flowers that I was seeing everywhere. Angier used a picture of the mature plant gone to seed, and I was seeing the young spring plant. They were both right, but it demonstrated the need to always learn plants by observing them in the field.

I began with the young mustard greens, chewing the raw leaves and enjoying the spicy flavor, despite the fine hairs covering the leaves (not all *Brassica* species are hairy). I then moved on to chopping the leaves up and adding them to salads, which was good. I then began to boil the leaves and serve them to my family, with butter. Everyone enjoyed them, even my father. Eventually I found that I could add mustard greens to just about any dish: soups, mixed salads, omelets, stir-fries, potatoes, you name it!

The flower buds and flowers have also been a good trail treat, and make a good, colorful garnish for salads and soups. I give them to children and tell them that they taste like broccoli, and most of the children say they enjoy the flowers.

The tender tops of the stems with the flower buds can also be snapped off the upper part of the plant, steamed, and served with sauce or cheese. The flavor is just like the Chinese broccoli that you buy at farmers' markets.

Lastly, you can come back to this annual plant in late fall, when the leaves are dried up and the tops are just tan-colored stems with small seedpods. Collect the pods in a bag, and break them up. The seeds go to the bottom of the bag, and you can discard the pod shells. The brown seeds are then used as a seasoning for various dishes calling for mustard, or you can try making your own mustard from them.

RECIPE

Pascal's Mustard

Fellow forager Pascal Baudar takes the pungent flowers of regular black mustard and grinds them while fresh, adding white wine and vinegar to taste. He thus produces a mustard condiment from the flowers—not the seeds, as is the usual custom. This makes a delicious mustard with a new twist.

SHEPHERD'S PURSE
Capsella bursa-pastoris

There are four species of *Capsella* worldwide, and only this one is found in Idaho.

Use: Leaves eaten raw or cooked; as medicine
Range: Prefers lawns, fields, and disturbed soils
Similarity to toxic species: None
Best time: Spring is best for greens; the seeds can be collected late spring to early summer.
Status: Somewhat common
Tools needed: A collection bag

Properties
Shepherd's purse, which is found all throughout the United States, is most easily identified by its flat, heart-shaped seedpods. They are unmistakable! The stalks rise about a foot or so tall. The little clusters of white flowers, sometimes tinged with a bit of purple, are formed in racemes along the stalk. These then mature into the heart-shaped pods. Trouble is, by the time you see all the seedpods, it's

Shepherd's purse leaves.

A view of the heart-shaped seed pods of shepherd's purse.

usually too late to use the young leaves for food, but now you know how to recognize shepherd's purse for the next season.

The young leaves are often hidden in the grass, making them somewhat inconspicuous. The basal leaves are toothed, with a large terminal lobe, typical of Mustard family leaves. The upper leaves are without a stalk and are more arrowhead-shaped. If you look closely, the young leaves will be covered with little hairs.

Uses

The flavor of shepherd's purse leaves is mild, and they could be used in just about any recipe, such as salads, sandwiches, soups, eggs, etc. However, they seem to be best when used in salads. Additionally, some Native Americans ground the seeds into a meal and used it in drinks and as a flour for various dishes.

Dr. Leonid Enari used to poll his students on which plant tasted best of the many wild

A view of the seeding stalk with the heart-shaped leaves.

plants he let them try. Consistently in his polls, shepherd's purse was rated the best. It is actually somewhat bland and peppery, but not too peppery, and the texture is mild. Even finicky eaters will like these leaves.

It's also very nutritious. About a half-cup of the leaves (100 grams) contains 208 milligrams (mg) of calcium, 86 mg of phosphorus, 40 mg of sodium, 394 mg of potassium, 36 mg of vitamin C, and 1,554 IU (international units) of vitamin A.

Dr. Enari told his students that this was the best plant to stop nosebleed. You boil the plant, dip a cotton ball into the water, and then apply to the nose. It turns out that many people have used this plant medicinally, especially to stop internal or external bleeding.

BITTERCRESS
Cardamine spp.

There are about 200 species of *Cardamine* worldwide, and fifteen can be found in Idaho. All are edible. The most common seem to be *C. hirsuta* and *C. oligosperma*.

Use: Leaves and all tender portions can be eaten.
Range: Common in the western United States, including parts of Idaho. Likes disturbed soils, especially common in gardens and nurseries.
Similarity to toxic species: None
Best time: Spring
Status: Widespread in localized areas
Tools needed: A collection bag

Properties

Bittercress can be very common in certain areas, mostly in gardens, where it appears as a common weed. The plant prefers moist and disturbed soils. It grows from sea level up to the foothills.

The small plant begins with a somewhat orderly appearing rosette of pinnately divided basal leaves. Each leaflet is generally round, all about the same size, though the terminal lobe is slightly larger—which is the case in just about all members of the Mustard family, except these leaves are very small. Each leaf can be about 2 inches long, with the terminal lobe about ½-inch wide.

One or more flower stalks may arise from the root. As the flower stalk arises, the leaves appearing on the stalk are similar, though the leaflets become more linear.

The bright white flowers appear mostly in the early spring and the early fall, though you can find the plant in flower nearly year-round. The flower pattern,

A view of the flowering and fruiting bittercress, growing in a pot.

like all members of the Mustard family, is four petals, four sepals, six stamens, and one pistil. The seedpods that follow the flowers are thin, like little needles, and an inch long, more or less.

Though somewhat short-lived, the plant can be collected anytime in its growing season. The little seedpods of this plant are known to pop open, throwing the seeds, which is why the plant can be found so abundantly within local areas.

Uses

If you have a garden, you've probably pulled *C. oligosperma* or *C. hirsuta* out of your pots and garden space, whether you knew its name or not. It's a small plant, it's an annual, and it spreads and spreads. Gardeners seem to hate it, even though they could eat it. Most gardeners and nurserymen I've talked to regard this as a serious nuisance plant, along with *Oxalis*. At least one person questioned why I would even consider including a plant such as this in a book of edible wild plants. "Because it's edible!" I replied.

The leaves are good raw when very young, and can be added to salads, soups, and various cooked dishes. They become just a bit stronger and bitter as they mature. In fact, any tender part of the plant can be added to a salad, soup, stew, or other cooked dish. The older leaves are edible too. They can have a stronger flavor, but cooking mellows them and makes them more palatable.

You would not want to make a whole meal from this plant, partly because

A view of the plant in the field.

The tiny bittercress plant, growing between ornamentals.

the leaves are so tiny that it takes a bit of time to gather a reasonable amount, and then it cooks down to very little bulk. But if you have this plant in abundance, you shouldn't overlook it. It's a nutritious, tasty addition to many dishes, as well as sandwiches. Consider it more of a garnish or spice when you add it to your meals. When in season and abundant, it's easy to collect several handfuls. Rinse the leaves to get rid of dirt, and add to your salad for a spicy addition.

I also find bittercress tasty when cooked like spinach, though it is a bit of work to collect enough for one pot of greens.

WATERCRESS
Nasturtium officinale

There are five species of *Nasturtium* worldwide, and only this one has been recorded in Idaho.

Use: Leaves eaten raw or cooked in salads, stir-fries, soup, etc.; can be dried for use as seasoning
Range: Restricted to the edges of lakes and streams
Similarity to toxic species: None
Best time: Summer, before the plant flowers; however, the plant can be collected anytime.
Status: Somewhat common along streams
Tools needed: A knife and a collection bag

Properties
Watercress is found worldwide along slow-moving streams and lakes, and is common in North America.

Once you learn to recognize watercress and see how the pinnately divided leaves are formed, you will find it quite easy to recognize, whether it is very young or older and flowering. First, it nearly always grows directly on the edges of streams where the water is slower. Occasionally you'll find it in sandy areas, but it is always an area that is at least seasonally underwater. You'll typically find it growing in thick mats.

A view of watercress at the edge of a stream.

Christopher collecting watercress. BARBARA KOLANDER

The leaves are pinnately divided into round leaflets. The stems are hollow, and there are white hairs on the underwater part of the stem. The plant is in the Mustard family, so when it gets older and flowers, the white flowers will be divided into the typical Mustard formula: four petals, four sepals, six stamens, and one pistil.

Though watercress can today be found worldwide, it is regarded by botanists as a native plant. It was known to be a part of the diet of early Native Americans.

Uses

Watercress was one of the very first wild plants that I learned how to identify and began to use. It is not only common throughout waterways in Idaho, but throughout the world.

I have always enjoyed making a salad of mixed greens, including watercress. But I don't usually make a salad with only watercress because it's a bit too spicy for my taste. A few raw watercress leaves are also tasty in sandwiches.

Watercress makes a delicious soup. Just finely chop the entire plant (tender stems and leaves) and add it to a water- or milk-based soup. Or you can add chopped watercress leaves to a miso base.

You can also cook the greens like spinach, serving them with a simple seasoning such as butter or cheese. Or, try mixing the greens into an egg omelet. If you're living off MREs or freeze-dried camping food, you can add some diced watercress to liven up your meals.

Also, for those of you who like making your own spices, you can dry and powder watercress and use it to season various dishes. Use it alone, or blend the powdered watercress with powdered seaweed or other flavorful herbs. You'll notice that some of the commercial salt-alternative spices use dried watercress leaves.

Another self-reliance idea is to dry wild foods into the basis of a soup stock, and then reconstitute later into a soup or stew broth. Dried and powdered watercress makes an ideal ingredient in such a mix.

Watercress has numerous medicinal applications. Some of the most popular, and most documented, include eating watercress to prevent eczema from returning, or for inflammatory flare-ups, as well as using an extract of watercress (obtained by boiling the leaves for ten minutes in water) as a disinfectant to wash the eczema area.

As a tea, watercress acts as a digestive aid, as the mustard oil glycosides, vitamins, and bitters in the tea promote production of the stomach juices that aid digestion. With its high potassium content, watercress tea assists the kidneys by acting as a diuretic, cleansing the urinary tract.

Watercress.

Cautions

If you have doubts about the purity of the water where you get your watercress, you should not eat it raw; boil it first and then use it in a cooked dish. Always wash watercress before using it. It grows right in the water, and you want to remove any dirt or other undesirables that may be clinging to the plant.

RECIPE

Saturday Night Special

Gently sauté half an onion bulb, diced, in a skillet with butter. You could substitute a handful of wild or garden onion greens. Quickly add at least 1 cup of watercress, chopped into large pieces, and cook gently until all is tender. Add a dash of soy sauce and serve.

HEDGE MUSTARD (TUMBLE MUSTARD)
Sisymbrium spp.

There are forty-one species of *Sisymbrium* worldwide, with four found in Idaho, all native to Europe. These are *S. altissimum, S. linifolium, S. loeselii,* and *S. officinale.*

Use: Leaves eaten raw or cooked
Range: Prefers disturbed soils of fields and farms, or along roadsides and trails
Similarity to toxic species: None
Best time: Spring
Status: Common
Tools needed: None

Properties
If you already know the mustards (*Brassica* spp.), you will very likely think "mustard" when you see a hedge mustard. The flowers of *Sisymbrium* tend to be smaller than the *Brassica* flowers, and the leaves tend to be more pointy compared to the rounder leaves of *Brassica.* Of course, to botanists, the distinction is mostly in the details of the flowers, but with sufficient observation, you'll be able to recognize the hedge mustards by leaf alone.

Uses
I think of the *Sisymbriums* as wild wasabi. Chew on a bit of the leaf, and you'll get that hot, horseradishy effect that opens your nostrils. I have friends who actually turn these leaves into a wild wasabi, which is great on sandwiches and crackers or as a dip. But, generally, I regard the hedge mustards as a source of very spicy greens that go well with salads, soups, egg dishes,

Hedge mustard flower and buds.

A maturing hedge mustard plant. Note the leaf shape.

A human-scale view of hedge mustard.

Someone else also likes the hedge mustard leaves.

sandwiches, stir-fries—just about any dish you can add greens to. These are spicy greens, in general a bit spicier than the greens of the common mustards (*Brassica*).

I have had broths made from the finely diced hedge mustard leaves, into which a lot of rice had been added. This dish was hot and good! I have also had "wild kimchi," which consisted of wild greens that had been marinated in raw apple cider vinegar. A lot of hedge mustard leaves were used in one of these kimchis, and it was delicious. You could also dry hedge mustard leaves and either reconstitute later, or just powder them and use as a seasoning.

The flowers are good too, but they aren't quite as good as the *Brassica* mustard flowers. Hedge mustard flowers seem to have too much of that bitter and astringent bite, so I use them sparingly in soups, salads, or other dishes.

CACTUS FAMILY (CACTACEAE)

There are 125 genera in the Cactus family, and about 1,800 species worldwide, mostly found in the American deserts. Three genera are found in Idaho.

According to Dr. Leonid Enari, the entire Cactus family is a very safe family for consumption. However, some are much too woody for food. A very few are extremely bitter—even after boiling—and you'd not even consider using them for food.

If you choose to experiment, just remember that palatability is the key. Don't eat any that are too woody, and any that are extremely bitter. Any that have a white sap when cut are not cacti, but lookalike members of the *Euphorbia* group.

PRICKLY PEAR
Opuntia spp.

At least three species of *Opuntia* (*O. columbiana, O. fragilis, O. polyacantha*) are found in the wild in Idaho. Nearly all species of *Opuntia* have a long history of being used for food.

A sprawling patch of the prickly pear cacti. LILY JANE TSONG

Use: Young pads for food, raw or cooked; fruits for desserts and juices; seeds for flour

Range: Hotter, drier parts of Idaho, from central river canyons southward

Similarity to toxic species: There is a *Euphorbia* which closely resembles the prickly pear. However, it lacks spines, and upon cutting, oozes a thick white sap. Do not eat such a plant.

Best time: Spring is the best time to collect the new pads, though the older ones can also be used. September through October is the best time for harvesting the fruits.

Status: Common

Tools needed: Metal tongs, sturdy bucket, possibly gloves

A bird makes its nest inside a cluster of prickly pear pads.

The youngest pads are easiest to clean for eating.

Properties

The prickly pear cacti are readily recognized by their flat to oval pads, with spines evenly spaced over their surfaces. The cacti flower by summer, and then the fruits mature by August and September.

The fruits tend to have more spines, so I collect those with metal tongs. Still using the tongs, I turn each fruit over in a flame—about ten seconds—to burn off the spines and glochids. Then I cut them in half, remove the fruit inside, and eat, preserve, or process in some way.

Uses

There are better cacti for eating than the species found in Idaho, but if you're stuck somewhere where cactus grows, one of these

A view of the ripe fruit.

might comprise a part of your meal. And there are several ways to get a meal from the prickly pear cactus: young pad, old pad, fruit, and seed.

The new growth of spring offers one of the more readily available foods, with the least amount of work. Remember, cacti all have some spines and tiny glochids, so you'll need to be careful whether you have the very young or the very old pads.

When you get the very young pads of spring, they will still be bright green and the tough outer layer won't yet have developed. Carefully pick, and then burn off the young spines, or thoroughly scrape each side to remove all spines and glochids. Then you can slice, or dice, and sauté to remove much of the liquid

FORAGER NOTE: If you collect cacti, you will, sooner or later, get spines and glochids in your skin. Spines are easy to see and relatively easy to remove. But glochids are smaller and hair-like, and more difficult to remove from the skin. Try smearing white glue on the part of your hand that has glochids. Let the glue dry. Now peel it off. This will usually remove most glochids.

and sliminess of the cacti. Cook off the water, and then add eggs, or potatoes, or even tofu for a delicious stew.

The fruits are delicious too—the closest thing to watermelon that you'll find in the wild, aside from the abundance of small seeds. An excellent drink is made by mixing 50 percent of this cactus fruit puree with 50 percent spring water.

Eating the prickly pear pads (raw, cooked, or juiced) has long been considered one way to combat diabetes. For those who don't want to grow their own, and clean their own, and cook their own *nopales*, you can now purchase the powder, which you can consume in various ways in order to combat diabetes. According to Dr. James Adams, "Cactus pads are excellent for people suffering from diabetes and helps with blood glucose levels. When fried, they taste like string beans."

Cautions

If you choose to collect these cacti for food, you will get spines and glochids in your skin, eventually. However, if you practice caution you can keep this inconvenience to a minimum.

Occasionally, people have experienced sickness after eating certain varieties. In some cases, this is due to a negative reaction to the mucilaginous quality. There may be other chemical reasons as well. So despite this being a very commonly used food historically for millennia, we suggest you start with very little and monitor your reactions.

BELLFLOWER FAMILY (CAMPANULACEAE)

There are seventy genera in this family, more or less, and about 2,000 species.

HAREBELLS
Campanula spp.

At least 300 species of *Campanula* are found in the Northern Hemisphere, and at least six are found in the Idaho territory.

Use: Primarily the roots for food
Range: Hills, mountains, fields
Similarity to toxic species: When the plant is not in flower and positive identification is not possible, many roots and bulbs can look very much alike. Therefore, never eat any of these unless you have established positive identification by observing the flowering plant.
Best time: These are easiest to find when flowering in the summer, though fall would be the best time.
Status: Common
Tools needed: Bag

A view of the beautiful harebell flower. BARBARA EISENSTEIN

Properties

Harebells typically grow in meadows and sparse forests at foothill elevations. Some are escaped from cultivation and will be found closer to towns. Most species are small, usually not rising more than 12 inches. The leaves are simple and alternate. In one case, *C. rotundifolia*, the first leaves are basal and ovate, and typically have died back by the time the plant blooms.

The flowers range from a light lavender to a deep blue, and rarely white. There are five petals, which are united to give the appearance of a bell.

A view of the harebell plant. BARBARA EISENSTEIN

Uses

The roots are dug and eaten. The size will vary, so just take the larger ones. Also, don't dig harebells up if there is not an abundance, since just one won't provide you with much food. On the other hand, the soil conditions in some areas will allow the harebells to grow larger roots, which are easily dug.

The roots are best cooked, such as boiling, adding to soups, or sautéing. The flavor is somewhat nut-like.

PINK FAMILY (CARYOPHYLLACEAE)

The Pink family consists of eighty-three to eighty-nine genera (depending on the authority), and about 3,000 species worldwide. At least twenty-eight genera are found in Idaho.

CHICKWEED
Stellaria media

There are 190 species of *Stellaria* worldwide, with at least eleven found in Idaho.

Use: The leaves are best raw in salads, but can also be cooked in various dishes or dried and powdered to make into pasta.
Range: Moist and shady areas in urban settings, mountain canyons, and along rivers. Scattered widely where the conditions are ideal.
Similarity to toxic species: See Cautions.
Best time: Spring; chickweed rarely lasts beyond midsummer.
Status: Common
Tools needed: None

Properties
Chickweed is one of the introduced *Stellarias* now widespread in Idaho. In fact, today it can be found worldwide, and all over the United States. It is common in urban yards, shady fields, and canyons. It is a short-lived annual that shrivels up by summer when the soil is dry.

Chickweed in flower.

Young chickweed in flower.

Chickweed is a low-growing, sprawling annual that first arises after the winter rains. The thin stem will grow up to a foot long, and upon close inspection, you'll see a line of fine white hairs along one side of the stem. The oval-shaped leaves, arranged in pairs along the stem, come to a sharp tip. The flowers are white and five-petaled, though it may appear to have ten petals because each flower has a deep cleft.

Uses

Chickweed is probably best used as a salad ingredient. In a thick patch of chickweed, you can cut off a handful of the stems just above the root. Then you just rinse the leaves, dice, and add salad dressing.

The plant can also be cooked in soups and stews. For those who are more adventurous, the entire chickweed plant (aboveground) can be dried, powdered, and mixed 50/50 with wheat flour, then run through a pasta machine. The result is a green pasta with a flavor of chickweed.

Young chickweed. Note flower buds.

Because chickweed grows close to the ground with fine stems, it is common to find other plants growing in chickweed patches. You need to make certain you are only collecting chickweed. We've seen poison hemlock growing within chickweed patches.

Cautions (for Chickweed)

You may find young common spurge (*Euphorbia peplus*) in chickweed patches, which superficially resembles chickweed, but spurge doesn't have the line of white hairs. Its stalk is more erect, and the leaves are alternate, not opposite like chickweed. If you break the stem of spurge, you will see a white sap; it shouldn't be eaten.

RECIPE

Mia's Chickweed Soup

Although chickweed can be found growing along city sidewalks, it's best to gather it in the wild, away from pesticides. As an homage to its humble origins, I call this my "Sidewalk Soup." It's simple, low fat (you can omit the pancetta or bacon and it's still amazing), and has a surprising depth of flavor reminiscent of spring peas and pea shoots. This is my version of "wild split-pea soup."

4–5 tablespoons diced pancetta (or you can use bacon)

1 medium onion, diced

1 stalk celery, diced

1 carrot, diced

1 teaspoon olive oil, as needed

4–5 cloves garlic, finely minced

1 teaspoon fennel seeds

1 small Oregon myrtle leaf

1 small leaf sage

2 teaspoons French or Italian herbs (I like oregano, thyme, and parsley)

1 small potato, cubed

6 cups packed chickweed, washed and chopped

1 teaspoon raw apple cider vinegar (to keep mixture green)

Salt and pepper to taste

In a heated stockpot, sauté the pancetta or bacon until crisp. Add onion, celery, and carrot, and sauté until translucent. You may need to add a bit of olive oil to the bottom of the pan, approximately 1 teaspoon. Add the garlic and spices and continue to sauté until just fragrant. Add the cubed potato; it will serve to thicken the soup once pureed. Add the chickweed (save a handful for garnish) and enough water to cover the chickweed with an inch of water. Cover and bring to a boil. Add the vinegar, then reduce to a light simmer for about 20–30 minutes.

Once slightly cooled, transfer to food processor and puree the mixture. Add salt and pepper to taste. Serve with tender, crisp chickweed as garnish. Delish!

—RECIPE FROM MIA WASILEVICH

GOOSEFOOT FAMILY (CHENOPODIACEAE)

The Goosefoot family consists of one hundred genera and about 1,500 species worldwide, found especially in deserts and saline or alkaline soils. Some members of the family are cultivated for food. Some botanists have lumped this family into Amaranthaceae.

According to Dr. Leonid Enari, this is one of those very promising plant families for food. His research indicated that most of the leaves could be used for food, either raw or cooked if too bitter and unpalatable. Dr. Enari also stated that the majority of the seeds could be harvested, winnowed, and ground for use as a flour or flour extender.

LAMB'S-QUARTER (WHITE AND GREEN)
Chenopodium album, C. murale

There are about one hundred species of *Chenopodium* worldwide, and eleven to fourteen species are found in Idaho.

Use: Leaves eaten raw or cooked; seeds added to soups or bread batter; leaves dried for seasoning

Range: Prefers disturbed soils of farms, gardens, hillsides, fields, along trails, etc.

Similarity to toxic species: Black nightshade leaves can be confused with lamb's-quarter leaves when very young. Be sure to look for the white, mealy (and "sparkly") underside of lamb's-quarter, and for the streak of red in the axils.

Best time: Spring for the leaves; late summer for the seeds

Status: Common and widespread

Tools needed: None

Properties

Lamb's-quarter is a plant that everyone has seen but probably not recognized. It is found all over North America (in fact, all over the world), and throughout Idaho. It's an annual plant that sprouts up in the spring and summer in fields, gardens, and disturbed soils, and generally grows about 3 to 4 feet tall. (I did record one at 12 feet, but that's the exception.)

The leaf shape is roughly triangular, somewhat resembling a goose's or duck's foot, hence the family name. The color of the stem and leaves are light green, and the axils of the leaves, and sometimes the stems, are streaked with red. The bottom of each leaf is covered with a mealy substance, causing raindrops to bead up on the leaf.

As the plant matures in the season, the inconspicuous green flowers will appear, and seeds will form as the plant dries and withers.

White lamb's-quarters. Note how rain beads up on the leaves.

A young white lamb's-quarter plant.

Ryan Swank inspects a field of lamb's-quarter.

A patch of the green lamb's-quarter.

Green lamb's-quarter, *C. murale*.

Uses

Lamb's-quarter is a versatile plant that can be used in many recipes. The young tender leaves can be cut into smaller pieces and used in a salad. The leaves and tender stems can be cooked like spinach and seasoned for a tasty dish. The water from this cooking makes a delicious broth. The leaves are a versatile green, which I've used as an addition to soups, egg dishes, and quiche, and even stir-fried with other vegetables.

FORAGER NOTE: Everyone should get to know lamb's-quarter. Not only is it widespread in Idaho, but it can also be found throughout the world. I once spent a week in the mountains eating only lamb's-quarter (salad, soup, fried, boiled). It is a plant that I can depend on finding even during a drought, when nothing else is available.

Lamb's-quarter will go to seed by late summer, and seeds from the dead plant are harvestable for several months. The seed is an excellent source of calcium, phosphorus, and potassium, according to the US Department of Agriculture. Collect the seeds by hand and place in a large salad bowl, then rub them between your hands to remove the chaff. Next, winnow them by letting handfuls drop into the salad bowl as you gently blow off the chaff. The seeds can then be added to soups, rice dishes, and bread batter.

Cautions
Older leaves may cause slight irritation to the throat when eaten raw, without dressing.

RECIPE

Breakfast in Boise

Cut a dozen seed heads about twelve inches long off a lamb's-quarter plant, strip off about two inches of the leaves and seeds for a handhold, then swirl the seed heads in a whipped egg or two, dust wet egg coating with flour, and then sauté. Season to taste, and serve with salsa, tortillas, and black beans. A traditional Native American dish that is excellent.

FORAGER NOTE: You've all heard of quinoa, right? It's a highly nutritious seed that has been used for thousands of years in Mexico and South America. Quinoa is *Chenopodium* quinoa, a "cousin" of our common lamb's-quarter! The leaves and seeds of both lamb's-quarter and quinoa are both tasty and nutritious.

RUSSIAN THISTLE
Salsola tragus, formerly *S. kali*

There are about one hundred species of *Salsola* worldwide. In Idaho, there are two species, and both of them are introduced. This plant is native to Central Asia and eastern Russia. The United States purchased flaxseed from Russia in 1874, and Russian thistle seed was in the flax. Russian thistle thus made its first appearance in North America in Scotland, South Dakota.

The overall Russian thistle plant, growing like a clump, blends into the landscape.

A view of the maturing Russian thistle plant; note the red in the axils.

A view of the flowering Russian thistle; note the inconspicuous flowers.

Use: The very young new growth can be cooked and eaten.

Range: Though seemingly a stereotypical plant of the desert, Russian thistle is somewhat widespread in valleys, fields, disturbed soils, and on the fringes of urban sprawl.

Similarity to toxic species: None

Best time: Spring

Status: Can be common locally and seasonally

Tools needed: A collection bag

Properties

Everyone seems to know Russian thistle (aka tumbleweed) from the Westerns: large, dry, round plants that blow across the plains in the wind. And while that is somewhat accurate, there is nothing edible when the plants mature into those large, dry balls.

It is the very young, new, and tender growth that can be used. The color of the stalk and leaves is pale green, almost a shade of blue, and the leaves are spiny and shaped like needles, maybe 1–2 inches in length. These leaves are covered with fine hairs, and you can usually observe some red in the axils and on the stalks.

Interestingly, this very inconspicuous plant produces an equally inconspicuous flower that is actually very beautiful if you take the time to observe it. The flowers are small and measure approximately ⅛–¼ inch across, and they consist of sepals that appear fragile and paper-like; there are no petals. These flowers are formed individually in the upper axils of the plant.

As the plant matures and gets older, it turns into a dry, round ball up to 3 feet in diameter, and when its small root is broken free by the wind, it rolls over the countryside and spreads as many as 200,000 winged seeds per plant. No wonder it's everywhere!

Uses

The main source of food here are the young, tender leaves. Collect them individually so you know they are still tender. I usually simply boil and serve with butter. They can also be served plain or with cheese.

Once boiled, taste the juice. It's actually a pretty good broth. You can drink it plain or use it as a soup base.

If I am mixing Russian thistle with other vegetables or greens, I will chop it up a bit first. If the leaves are tender enough, they could be boiled, then mixed into a casserole or even a meatloaf-type dish.

Sometimes, if you get the very young shoots of the Russian thistle, you can quickly dip them into boiling water to reduce their fibrous surfaces. They can then be used in raw dishes without experiencing any irritation to the throat.

RECIPE

Tumbled Rice

Cook 1 cup of rice (use good rice, like wild rice or long-grained brown rice) according to the package instructions. Separately cook about 2 cups of tender Russian thistle leaves, and about 1 cup of hedge mustard leaves. When all is cooked, blend them together while still hot. Give the dish a bit of garlic powder to taste, and top with shredded Jack cheese before serving.

STONECROP FAMILY (CRASSULACEAE)

There are thirty genera and about 1,500 species worldwide. Four of those genera are found in Idaho.

STONECROP
Sedum spp.

A view of the stonecrop plant. BARBARA EISENSTEIN

There are about 450 species of Sedum worldwide, and approximately ten have been recorded in Idaho.

Use: Food, water
Range: Open rocky places
Similarity to toxic species: None
Best time: May through summer
Status: Somewhat common
Tools needed: A collection bag

PROPERTIES

This is a low-growing, creeping succulent, with alternately arranged spear-shaped leaves that are somewhat flattened in cross-section. Flowers are yellow, star-shaped, and arranged in compact cymes. There are four to five sepals, free or fused; four to five petals, and eight or ten stamens. Often found growing in the cleavage of rocks, this is very much the type of plant you'd expect to be used in landscaping. It can be found, in the appropriate areas, from Canada to Mexico.

Uses

Stonecrop leaves are mostly used as a trail nibble, especially when water is needed. The succulent leaves are mild early in the season, but become tough and astringent as they age.

The plant is small and grows slowly, so practice conservation when you decide to try these. Don't uproot the plant, since you're only going to be pinching off the leaves as a nibble.

You can try mixing stonecrop leaves with other salad ingredients. You might also try a small salad with only the stonecrop leaves and some dressing. These leaves will also do well in various cooked dishes, such as stews or soups, though when cooked they are mostly bland.

This native would lend itself well to native gardens, where you grow your native foods in your own backyard. A stem of the plant, with leaves still attached, can be planted directly into appropriate soil and it will grow. Some gardeners have reported that it also grows easily from seed, though in good garden soil the stonecrop can get out-competed and overgrown by other plants.

HEATH FAMILY (ERICACEAE)

The Heath family contains about one hundred genera and 3,000 species worldwide. In Idaho, there are seventeen genera of this family.

KINNIKINNICK
Arctostaphylos uva-ursi

There are sixty-two species of *Arctostaphylos* worldwide, with at least two found in Idaho.

Use: Leaves used as tea or smoked; fruits eaten or made into a cider
Range: Found widely throughout Idaho, in prairies, dry alpine meadows, dry coniferous forest, etc. Found from Alaska south to California and New Mexico, and east to the Atlantic coast.
Similarity to toxic species: None
Best time: Summer for the fruits
Status: Relatively common
Tools needed: Basket for collecting

Properties
Kinnikinnick is a low-growing shrub, with its stems trailing across ground, rarely rising more than half a foot off the ground. The leathery leaves are alternately

A view of the sprawling kinnikinnick. BARRY BRECKLING

A view of the kinnikinnick plant. ALGIE AU

arranged, dark green, and rounded at the tip. They are about an inch long, more or less. Flowers are light pink, urn-shaped in small clusters near the tips of stems, very typical of this family. The bright red berries—which follow the flowers—are less than a half-inch across.

Uses

Kinnikinnick berries are edible, often added to other foods. One botanist wrote that the fruit "tastes like lint," which certainly doesn't sound appealing. In fact they are dry, with a bland, almost sour flavor. Sometimes, you can detect a hint of sweetness. I like them.

Various Northwestern tribes (and tribes throughout kinnikinnick's range) have used the berries for food, typically added to other fruits as well as mixtures including eggs and meats. Think of them as a mild sweetening agent, and they are best when mixed with other foods. Daniel Moerman, in his *Native American Ethnobotany*, lists uses of these fruits rather extensively, and includes desserts, drinks, fried dishes, ice cream, berry dishes, sauces, and main courses all using the kinnikinnick berries.

My favorite recipe involves soaking the mashed berries in warm water, not exactly cooking them, and letting them simmer for half an hour or so. Then I strain out the liquid and sweeten with just a bit of honey. This makes a very tasty trail cider.

FORAGER NOTE: "Kinnikinnick" is an Algonquian term that was originally applied to this plant, referring to something that was mixed, in this case a smoking mix. The term refers to any of the plants that were smoked, usually this one, along with some willow barks, dogwood, and others. The term has sometimes been used to refer to any nontobacco smoking mix.

These fruits are usually not very abundant, and though they can be cooked into a tasty dish when somewhat abundant, these are more likely to be just a trail nibble.

Kinnikinnick is probably most well known as a traditional alternative to tobacco. It was used as a smoke in the "old days," typically mixed with other substances such as dogwood or willow bark. Some have ascribed mild narcotic effects to these leaves, and while that may be so, I have simply enjoyed them as a pleasant smoke in my pipe without all the harmful effects of commercial tobacco. Different groups had their own preferred mixes, and I suggest you simply try your own experiments until you find what you like. By itself, kinnikinnick doesn't have a strong flavor or aroma, so I have tried various mixes, using other substances as willow bark, mint leaves, mullein leaves, mugwort, and sometimes various sages.

The leaves are leathery, and when dried, they become brittle, so you will need to crush them into smaller pieces before you can put them into your pipe. Sometimes, I blend kinnikinnick with various other herbs in my electric coffee grinder to get a homogenous blend.

The leaves are also used as a tea, made by infusion. Moerman lists dozens of ways in which indigenous peoples of the Northwest and elsewhere used the leaves (usually an infusion from the leaves) to heal wounds. He lists many other similar medicinal applications.

Lewis and Clark

Lewis and Clark described seeing the kinnikinnick in bloom several times, which they referred to by the name *Sackacommis*.

A view of the kinnikinnick plant. ALGIE AU

HUCKLEBERRY AND BLUEBERRY
Vaccinium spp.

The *Vaccinium* genus includes more than 400 species worldwide, with at least eleven recorded in Idaho. In general, *Vacciniums* are often referred to as huckleberries, blueberries, cranberries, and even bilberries, depending on the species. Nearly all are native here, except *V. macrocarpon*, which is the common cranberry, native to eastern North America.

Use: The fruits are edible.
Range: *Vacciniums* are forest inhabitors found mostly in woodland clearings and in the woods themselves, mostly coniferous woods. They like moist, shaded areas and north-facing hills.
Similarity to toxic species: None
Best time: Early spring for flowers; early summer for fruit
Status: Common
Tools needed: Collecting basket

Properties
These are shrubs, with alternate evergreen to deciduous leaves that are broadly lance-shaped. The stems are trailing to erect. The flower's petals generally number four to five, with a corolla that is cup- or urn-shaped. The fruit can be red

Huckleberry in fruit. ZOYA AKULOVA

or blue, larger or smaller, and has flattened ends. Generally, the plants with the most desirable fruits are the smaller shrubs, about 3 feet tall, with the larger, sweet, juicy, blue berries measuring about ¼- to ½-inch in diameter.

The fruits of all *Vaccinium* can be eaten, and some are better than others. The best way to make sure you have identified the plant is to observe it when the plant is fruiting, and then take note of the leaf and stem characteristics.

Many species grow in the Northwest, and they are loosely categorized into three groups: those that are found in the bogs and swamps; those that produce the tiny (usually) red berries, which are very sweet but require a lot of time to collect in any appreciable amount (for example, *V. scorparium* or whortleberry); and those that grow in the higher elevations where there is well-drained soil, with dark blue berries, such as *V. globulare*.

Blueberry (*V. uliginosum*). JEAN PAWEK

BOG BLUEBERRY
Vaccinium uliginosum

The fruits of all species can be eaten raw or cooked. The flavor of the ripe fruit can vary from tart to very sweet. They can be used to makes pies and jellies, cobblers, and preserves. The fruits can also be dried for later use and used to make a fruit pemmican.

The dried leaves can be infused to make a tasty and nutritious tea.

GERANIUM FAMILY (GERANIACEAE)

Worldwide, there are six genera and about 750 species in this family. In Idaho, this family is represented by two genera.

FILAREE
Erodium cicutarium

There are about seventy-four species of *Erodium* worldwide, and two are found in Idaho, *E. cicutarium* and *E. ciconium*.

Use: The leaves are eaten raw, cooked, or juiced.

Range: Prefers lawns, fields, cultivated and disturbed soils, and the fringes of the urban wilderness

Similarity to toxic species: Since filaree superficially resembles a fern, and perhaps a member of the Carrot or Parsley families (when not in flower), make sure you are thoroughly familiar with filaree before eating any.

Best time: Spring

Status: Somewhat common

Tools needed: A collection bag

Properties

Filaree is a very common urban weed, found in gardens, grasslands, and fields. This annual plant grows as a low-growing rosette of pinnately compound leaves, which are covered with short hairs. The stalk is fleshy. Sometimes people think they are looking at a fern when they see filaree. The small five-petaled flowers of spring are purple, followed by the very characteristic needlelike fruits.

The flower of filaree. RICK ADAMS

Note the linear seed capsules of filaree.

An overall view of the filaree plant.

Uses

Filaree leaves and stalks can be picked when young and enjoyed in salads. The leaves are a little fibrous, but sweet. I pick the entire leaf, including the long stem, for salads or other dishes. They are best chopped up before being added to salads or cooked dishes such as soups or stews.

You might also enjoy simply picking the tender stems and chewing on them. They are sweet and tasty, somewhat reminiscent of celery. In fact, sometimes in a dry year, I find the stem is the only part I will eat. The leafy section is drier and more fibrous, and lends itself better to being added to a stew.

In wet seasons, the spring growth of filaree is more succulent and tasty. In dry years, the season will be short and the leaves and stems of filaree will be less desirable.

RECIPE

Filaree-Up My Cup

If you have a wheatgrass juicer, you can process filaree leaves and then enjoy the sweet green juice without the fiber.

GOOSEBERRY FAMILY (GROSSULARIACEAE)

This family includes only the *Ribes* genus. There are 120 species worldwide, and some found all over the United States. At least twenty-three species are recorded in Idaho, not including varieties.

CURRANT AND GOOSEBERRY
Ribes spp.

Use: The fruits are eaten raw, dried, or cooked/processed into juice, jam, and jelly.

Range: Found in the mountains, in flat plains, along rivers, etc.

Similarity to toxic species: When seeing currants for the first time, some folks think they're looking at poison oak—they've heard the saying "Leaflets three, let it be." But the currant has three lobes per leaf, not three distinct leaflets, as does poison oak.

Best time: The fruits are available in midspring.

Status: Common

Tools needed: None

Properties

Currants and gooseberries are both the same genus, and so we'll treat them together. Both are low shrubs, mostly long vining shoots that arise from the base. The gooseberries have thorns on the stalks and fruits, and the currants do not.

A view of the ripe fruit. KYLE CHAMBERLAIN

Currant in fruit. HELEN W. NYERGES

The leaves look like little three- to five-fingered mittens. The fruits of both currants and gooseberries hang from the stalks, with the withered flower usually still adhering to the end of the fruit.

You will find currants or gooseberries throughout the diverse ecosystems of Idaho.

Uses

Though the straight shoots of currants make excellent arrow shafts, currants and gooseberries are mostly regarded as a great fruit, either eaten raw as a snack, or dried, or cooked into various recipes.

Gooseberries are a bit more work to eat since they're covered with tiny spines. I have mashed them and then strained the pulp through a sieve or fine colander. Then I used the fruit as a jelly for pancakes.

Ripe and ripening currant fruits.

The leaves from the emerging stalk of currant.

Currants require no preparation, so they can be picked off the stalks and eaten fresh. But make sure they are ripe—they'll be a bit tart otherwise.

In the old days, the currant was a valuable fruit, dried and powdered and added to dried meats as a sugar preservative. Today, you can just dry the fruits into simple trail snacks. Or you can collect a lot and make jams or jellies, or even delicious drinks. And though the currant leaf is not usually regarded as an important food source, some can be eaten in salads or cooked dishes for a bit of

Gooseberry. HELEN WONG

Gooseberry. HELEN WONG

Ripe currants.

vitamin C. They are slightly tough as they get older.

Rule of thumb on the *Ribes* fruits: If it tastes good, it's good to eat. None are poisonous, but not all are palatable. Remember, some of the forest species are generally not terribly palatable and some are without significant pulp.

Cautions
Be sure you've identified currant or gooseberry, and that you can tell the difference between these and poison oak.

Lewis and Clark
On April 16, 1805, Meriwether Lewis wrote, "Among others there is a currant which is now in blume and has yellow blossom something like the yellow currant of the Missouri but it is a different species." Botanists believe that Lewis was describing *R. aureum.* Lewis also writes, "I find these fruits very pleasant particularly the yellow currant which I think vastly preferable to those of our gardens . . . The fruit is a berry . . . It is quite as transparent as the red current of our gardens, not so ascid, & more agreeably flavored."

WALNUT FAMILY (JUGLANDACEAE)

The Walnut family contains nine genera and about sixty species worldwide. In Idaho, it is represented by the *Carya* genus (hickory), and the *Juglans* genus.

Black Walnut
Juglans spp.

There are twenty-one recorded species of *Juglans* worldwide, and four of those species are found in Idaho.

Use: The nutmeat is eaten. The green walnuts are used as fish stunner and the black hulls used as a dye.
Range: Scattered in lower elevation canyons, valley farmland, and urban areas
Similarity to toxic species: None
Best time: Nuts mature in mid- to late summer.
Status: Occasional exotic
Tools needed: Gloves suggested

Properties
In Idaho, there are four introduced species of *Juglans*, including the English walnut.

Note the thick shells of the black walnut; sometimes the meat is minimal.

The black walnut is widespread in Idaho's canyons, valleys, and hillsides. In addition, you might encounter the English walnut (*J. regia*), either planted in yards or surviving around old farms and cabins.

This is a full-bodied native deciduous tree with pinnately divided leaves. There are typically eleven to nineteen leaflets per leaf.

You know what the English walnut you buy in the store looks like; this one is similar but there are some important differences. First, all the black walnuts are smaller. They have a soft green outer layer, which turns black as it matures and has long been used as a dye. The shell of the English walnut is thin and easy to crack, but approximately one-half of the black walnut is shell. The nut requires a rock or a hammer to crack. The meat in the black walnut is oily and delicious, though there's not as much meat as you'll find in the cultivated English walnut.

Uses

Yes, these are walnuts! But unlike the more commonly cultivated English walnut, black walnuts are more like the hickory nuts of eastern states. The shells are hard and thick.

A view of the walnut leaf and unripe fruit.

Some mature black walnuts in a tree.

Note that black walnuts are covered in a fleshy material that dries when the walnuts are mature and fall. This outer black covering is an excellent dye or pigment material for arts and crafts, but you want to consider wearing gloves when collecting. I once used this to paint children's faces at a day camp, and since the dye takes about two weeks to wash off, I heard from several unhappy parents.

Once you crack open the walnut, you can pick out the edible meat and eat it as is, or add it to bread products, cookies, cakes, even stews and meat dishes. It is a very tasty, oil-rich food, and quite a delicacy, but it just takes a lot of work to get to it.

Immature walnuts are sometimes pickled as well. You boil the walnuts, and change the water a few times. Then you pack them into jars with vinegar and pickling spices. For details on how to do this properly, read *The New Wildcrafted Cuisine* by Pascal Baudar.

Also, the immature green walnuts were one of the substances used in the old days to capture fish. Indigenous peoples would crush the green walnuts and toss them into pools of water, or the edges of slow-moving streams, and the fish would float to the top. The fish would be scooped out with nets, and then everyone would have dinner!

MINT FAMILY (LAMIACEAE)

The Mint family has about 230 genera and about 7,200 species worldwide. In Idaho, we have examples from twenty-seven genera, many of which are food and medicine.

MINT
Mentha spp.

There are eighteen species of *Mentha* worldwide, with five recorded in the wild in Idaho.

Use: As a beverage
Range: Along rivers and wet areas; often cultivated and escaped from cultivation
Similarity to toxic species: None
Best time: Mint can be collected at any time.
Status: Not common
Tools needed: A collection bag

Properties

Our wild mints in Idaho include spearmint (*M. spicata*), peppermint (*M. piperita*), and field mint (*M. arvensis*). In the wild, mints are typically found along streams. They are sprawling, vining plants with squarish stems and finely wrinkled opposite leaves. Crush the leaf for the unmistakable clue to identification. If you have a good sense of smell, you'll detect the obvious minty aroma.

Peppermint and spearmint are usually cultivated in gardens. They sometimes escape cultivation and are found in marshes, ditches, meadows, around lakes, and in other moist areas.

The white, pink, or violet flowers of *Mentha* are clustered in tight groups along the stalk, often appearing like balls on the stems. The

Wild mint. Note the opposite leaves and square stem.

Wild mint. JEFF MARTIN

flowers, though five-petaled, consist of an upper two-lobed section and a lower three-lobed section.

Uses

The wild mints are not primarily a food, but are excellent sources for an infused tea. Put the fresh leaves into a cup or pot, boil some water, and then pour the water over the leaves. Cover the cup and let it sit a while. I enjoy the infusion plain, but you might prefer to add honey or lemon or some other flavor.

A close-up of a wild mint.

We've had some campouts where we had very little food, and were relying on fishing and foraged food. Even in off-seasons in the mountains, we were able to find wild mint and make a refreshing tea. The aroma is invigorating, and helps to open the sinuses. The flavor and taste of mint tea seems even more enjoyable when camping. Also, you can just crush some fresh leaves and add them to your canteen while hiking. It makes a great cold trail beverage, and requires no sweeteners.

Sometimes, we add the fresh leaves to trout while it is cooking. They add a great flavor. If used sparingly, you can dice up the fresh leaves and add them to salads for a refreshing minty flavor. Of course, they can be diced and added to various dessert dishes, like ice cream, sherbet, etc. Or you can try adding a few sprigs of mint to your soups and stews to liven up the flavor. And if you really want to try something special at your doomsday parties, add a little fresh mint to your favorite pouch of MRE.

If you have a mildly upset stomach, try some mint tea before reaching for some fizzy pill. Mint tea has a well-deserved reputation for calming an upset stomach. The Ojibwa people used the tea to help reduce fevers.

MALLOW FAMILY (MALVACEAE)

The Mallow family includes 266 genera and about 4,025 species worldwide. There are nine genera represented in Idaho, including hibiscus.

According to Dr. Leonid Enari, the Mallow family is a safe family for wild-food experimentation. He cautions, however, that some species may be too fibrous to eat.

The round leaves of mallow and the young seeds.

MALLOW
Malva neglecta

There are thirty to forty species of *Malva* worldwide. *Malva* is widespread in North America, with four species found in Idaho.

Use: Leaves raw, cooked, or dried (for tea); "cheeses" eaten raw or cooked; seeds cooked and eaten like rice
Range: Urban areas such as fields, disturbed soils, and gardens
Similarity to toxic species: None
Best time: Spring
Status: Common and widespread
Tools needed: A collection bag

Properties
The plants resemble geraniums with their rounded leaves. Each leaf's margin is finely toothed, and there is a cleft at the middle of the leaf to which the long stem is attached. If you look closely, you'll see a red spot where the stem meets the leaf.

The flowers are small but attractive, composed of five petals, generally colored white to blue, though some could be lilac or pink. The flowers are followed by the round flat fruits, which gave rise to the plant's other name, "cheeseweed."

These plants are widespread, mostly in urban terrain and on the fringes.

Uses
When you take a raw leaf and chew on it, you will find it becomes a bit mucilaginous. For this reason, it is used to soothe a sore throat. In Mexico, you can find the dried leaf under the Spanish name *malva* at herb stores, sold as a medicine.

Though the entire plant is edible, the stalks and leaf stems tend to be a bit fibrous, so I just use the leaf and discard the stem. These are good added to salads, though they are a bit tough as the only salad ingredient.

Mallow leaves.

A close-up of the mallow seeds.

The mallow leaf is also good in cooked dishes—soups, stews, or finely chopped for omelets and stir-fries. I have even seen some attempts to use larger mallow leaves as a substitute for grape leaves in dolmas, which are cooked rice wrapped in grape leaves. I thought it worked out pretty well.

As this plant flowers and matures, the flat and round seed clusters appear. When still green, these make a good nibble. The green "cheeses" (as they are commonly called) can be added raw to salads, cooked in soups, or even pickled into capers. Once the plant is fully mature and the leaves are drying up, you can collect the now-mature cheeses. The round clusters will break up into individual seeds, which you can winnow and then cook like rice. Though the cooked seeds are a bit bland, they are reminiscent of rice. Because mallow is so very common, it would not be hard to prepare a dish of the mallow seed. To really improve the flavor, try mixing the mallow seeds with quinoa, buckwheat groats, or couscous.

The root of the related marsh mallow (*Althaea officinalis*) was once the source for making marshmallows, which are now just another junk food. Originally, the roots were boiled until the water was gelatinous. The water would be whipped to thicken it and then sweetened. You'd then have a spoonful to treat a cough or sore throat. Yes, you can use the common mallow's roots to try this, though it doesn't get quite as thick as the original.

MINER'S LETTUCE FAMILY (MONTIACEAE)

The Miner's Lettuce family includes twenty-two genera with about 230 species worldwide. There are at least seven genera represented in Idaho.

Dr. Leonid Enari regarded this as a completely safe family for wild-food experimentation. He taught that all members could be eaten, usually raw, but sometimes needed to be steamed or cooked for improved palatability. Dr. Enari also taught that the seeds of most could be harvested and eaten.

SPRING BEAUTY
Claytonia lanceolata

There are twenty-seven species of *Claytonia* worldwide, with twelve recorded in Idaho (not including subspecies). Many species are found throughout forest habitats: *C. arenicola, C. cordifolia, C. lanceolata, C. megarhiza, C. parviflora, C. perfoliata, C. rubra,* and *C. sibirica.* This genus was formerly referred to as *Montia.*

Use: The entire plant, including the bulbs, can be eaten.
Range: Widespread from Canada, east to the Rockies, south to central California. In Idaho, expect to find it mostly in open fields and higher elevation meadows.
Similarity to toxic species: None
Best time: Spring. It's one of the first spring plants that can be eaten.
Status: Relatively common
Tools needed: Bag for leaves, trowel for tubers

Properties

Spring beauty is a perennial herb that grows no more than about 6 inches tall. There is a little root, like a small radish, up to an inch in diameter. One or more stalks will grow from each little bulb.

The leaves are all more or less basal, appearing in the spring and summer. The linear to lance-shaped leaves are about 2½ to 4 inches long, and they are arranged opposite each other. Remember, this is related to miner's lettuce, and the color, texture, and feel of the spring beauty leaf is very much like that of its relative. The small white flowers often have pink veins and are about 5 to 12 millimeters wide.

Spring beauty is found mostly in subalpine areas, even at the edges of snow-melt. This is a wilderness plant, not one you'll find in urban fields or in your backyard. Once, however, when pulled over to the side of the road at a high-elevation location, I found spring beauty growing in a little patch of moist soil between the road and the abutting mountain.

The spring beauty plant. KEIR MORSE

Uses

Spring beauty leaves are pleasant to all palates and can be used as a main salad ingredient or mixed with other greens. They are also great just cooked like spinach. You can try them in egg dishes and soups. The flavor is mild and the texture is spinach-like, so these greens will go well with most dishes.

The little starchy bulbs can be dug, but I generally just leave them alone. In heavily traveled areas, I have seen certain wild foods "dry up" until the area has had a chance to recover. Yes, these bulbs are good—mild, tasty, and nutritious. The bulbs are down about 6 inches at least, and you can carefully dig them out with a little trowel.

But be an ecological forager. Don't deplete a patch, and do your best to keep the area looking natural, leaving it better than you found it!

Lewis and Clark

The Lewis and Clark expedition passed along the Columbia River and dipped into Oregon. According to the journal kept by Captain Lewis, in an entry dated June 25, 1806: "I met with a plant the root of which the Shoshones eat. It is a small knob root a good deel in flavor an consistency like the Jerusalem artichoke." He was speaking of the spring beauty tubers.

MINER'S LETTUCE
Claytonia perfoliata

SIBERIAN MINER'S LETTUCE
Claytonia sibirica

There are twenty-seven species of *Claytonia* worldwide, with twelve found in Idaho (not including subspecies). This genus was formerly referred to as *Montia*.

Use: The entire aboveground plant can be eaten raw, boiled, steamed, sautéed, or added to soup, eggs, etc.
Range: Mostly found in moist canyons below 3,000 feet, with *C. perfoliata* more common
Similarity to toxic species: None
Best time: Spring
Status: Common seasonally
Tools needed: A collection bag

Properties
Miner's lettuce leaves are formed in a rosette, with each leaf arising from the root. The young leaves are linear, and the older ones are somewhat triangular to quadrangular in shape, with some appearing water-spotted. The key characteristic is the flowering stalk with its pink or white five-petaled flowers, which arise from a cup-shaped leaf. Clusters of these unique cup-shaped leaves, all arising from a common root, like a head of leaf lettuce, make this a very easy plant to recognize.

Miner's lettuce. RICK ADAMS

Very young miner's lettuce.

A view of young miner's lettuce.

Miner's lettuce was one of the very first wild foods that I learned to identify. I'd seen the characteristic leaf—a round cuplike leaf with the flower stalk growing out of the middle—in Bradford Angier's *Free for the Eating*. It was just one drawing, but I was certain I'd be able to recognize it. One day I got a phone call from a fellow budding forager, and he told me that he'd spotted the plant in the local mountains. I bicycled to the site that afternoon, climbed up the hillside, and sure enough, I found it!

That night I tried my first miner's lettuce in salad, and also some boiled like spinach. It was good, but perhaps the experience was a bit anticlimactic because I was so wrapped up in the lore and history of the plant. I didn't realize there'd be nothing really incredible about the plant—just a tasty though somewhat bland leaf that could be used in many ways.

Uses

It seems that everyone knows miner's lettuce. This is probably because the plant is so distinctive—when it's in flower, you really can't confuse it for something else. Plus, it tastes good, it often grows very abundantly, and it's easy to work with. Think of the plant as a somewhat succulent lettuce that is also good cooked, and you'll get some idea how versatile this plant can be.

Flavor- and texture-wise, this is perhaps one of my favorite wild foods. My brother Richard always regarded it as his favorite. We have used it in many recipes—just think of all the diverse ways in which we use common spinach!

To give some examples of the many ways in which we can eat miner's lettuce, consider a weekend survival trip I once led for a dozen young men. Our only food was what we fished or foraged, and there was very little growing in the area besides miner's lettuce. We had miner's lettuce salad, miner's lettuce soup, fried miner's lettuce, boiled miner's lettuce, miner's lettuce cooked with fish, and

A huge miner's lettuce leaf.
GARY GONZALES

miner's lettuce broth! If we were in a kitchen with all sorts of condiments, we'd have had miner's lettuce omelets, and soufflés, and stir-fries, and green drinks.

In other words, in any recipe—raw, cooked, or juiced—that calls for "greens," you can use miner's lettuce.

RECIPE

Richard's Salad

This is my brother Richard's recipe. He lived in Portland for part of the year, working as a welder for the Rose Festival, and made miner's lettuce salads whenever possible in the spring.

Rinse 4 cups of miner's lettuce leaves. Mix with a dressing of equal parts cold-pressed olive oil and raw apple cider vinegar, to which you can add a dash of garlic powder and paprika, to taste. Richard sometimes topped his salad with sliced hard-boiled eggs.

BITTERROOT
Lewisia rediviva

About eighteen species of *Lewisia* are known in North America, and at least six (not including varieties) are recorded in Idaho.

Use: The root is eaten.
Range: Ridges, barren areas, sagebrush plains
Similarity to toxic species: None
Best time: Spring
Status: Sensitive; sometimes locally abundant
Tools needed: Digging tool

Properties

Get to know the common bitterroot and you should be able to recognize all varieties. In general, most have pink or white flowers.

The conspicuous flower appears to grow all by itself, at ground level. By the time it flowers, the leaves have typically already withered. The flowers of *R. rediviva* consist of twelve to eighteen pink to white petals, each of which is somewhat fleshy. There are many stamens, and four to eight styles. The similar flowers of *R. columbiana* consists of six to eleven petals. There are also six to nine sepals, which are oval-shaped and colored green to red-toned. The mostly basal leaves are linear-oblanceolate, in a basal rosette. They tend to be all withered by the

A view of the young plant. JEAN PAWEK

A view of the flowering plant. BARBARA EISENSTEIN

time the flowers develop. The roots are fleshy and radiating, and cormose, with a reddish-brown skin. The root and caudex are short and thick. The plant is found on rocky slopes and crevices in the sagebrush plains to the lower mountains. You might not see it unless you're practically right on top of it.

Uses
The genus name comes from Captain Meriwether Lewis of the Lewis and Clark Expedition of 1804 to 1806. The expedition found Native Americans of the High Plains eating bitterroot, so named because they are bitter, especially if eaten after they flower. They should be collected before flowering, and the skin of the roots should be thoroughly removed. They are also best if boiled or baked. Bitterroot lends a mucilaginous property to dishes cooked with it.

To the native people of the area, the bitterroot was an important historical food. Depending on when you collect it, it could still provide you with a meal after a bit of work. The Montana Salish still have bitterroot harvests and feeds to this day.

This seems like an important plant to know about for historical reasons, though we're big fans of just admiring these plants and leaving them alone!

Lewis and Clark

On August 22, 1805, Lewis wrote about George Drouillard acquiring some dried bitterroots from the Indians whose territory they were passing through. He said that the roots were "cylindric and as white as snow throughout, except some small parts of the hard black rind which they had not separated in the prepera-tion. This the Indians with me informed were always boiled for use. I made the experiment, found that they became perfectly soft by boiling, but had a very bit-ter taste, which was naucious to my palate, and I transferred them to the Indians who had eat them heartily."

MULBERRY FAMILY (MORACEAE)

Mulberry is a member of the Mulberry Family, which includes thirty-seven genera and 1,100 species worldwide.

MULBERRY
Morus alba

The genus *Morus* includes about twelve species worldwide. In Idaho, the genus *Morus* is represented by *Morus alba*, the white mulberry, most commonly found in the wild, and *Morus rubra*.

Use: Edible fruit
Range: In the wild, you'll find the white mulberry in disturbed soils, on the edges of streams, in moist areas, and in cultivated areas.
Similarity to toxic species: None
Best time: Summer
Status: Somewhat common in its ideal sites
Tools needed: Basket or box. Fruits are fragile so don't use a bag.

Properties

Mulberry is a tree, with alternate leaves, unlobed or three- to five-lobed. The tree produces a catkin, and then a fruit that resembles an elongated blackberry. The fruit is technically referred to as a fruit of many achenes ("seeds") within the fleshy calyces. Just think elongated blackberry and you'll get the picture. The white mulberry fruits are white to pink, and the black mulberries are purple.

Uses

Pick mulberries and use them right away. They are best very fresh.

If you go to a nursery to buy a fruiting mulberry tree, you might not find one. Some years ago, nurserymen started switching to nonfruiting varieties because, according to gardeners and homeowners, "The fruits stain the sidewalks." Yes, that happens!

Where I once lived, there was large old mulberry just outside the back door, and yes, it regularly stained the cement walkway. These were white mulberries, and the stains weren't permanent. I tried to pick and eat as many as I could, and the neighborhood squirrels usually beat me to the fruit on the path.

Mulberries have long been planted as a landscape and park tree, though they have fallen out of favor because of the staining of sidewalks. Sometimes the fruiting varieties are planted on large properties so that the fruit attracts the birds.

The fruits of any variety can be collected when fresh and eaten as is. They can be dried too, but the fruit always seems fragile and is best eaten right away.

A view of the leaf and fruit.

A view of the white mulberry.

The fruit of the mulberry. ISTOCK.COM

Of course, jams, jellies, and preserves can be made with mulberries, so you have some later in the year.

Could the mulberry be regarded as a "clothing tree"? Recall, this is the only thing that silk moths will eat. I remember a grammar school experiment where we got silk moths from somewhere, and fed them mulberry leaves in our classroom. We actually picked the leaves from the school yard. Everyone talked about how we'd unroll some of the silk and make a scarf or shirt, but we never got beyond just feeding the larvae. Additionally, archers consider the long straight branches of the mulberry tree one of the ideal woods for carving a bow.

EVENING PRIMROSE FAMILY (ONAGRACEAE)

The Evening Primrose family has twenty-two genera and about 657 species worldwide. There are twenty genera of this family in Idaho.

FIREWEED
Chamerion angustifolium

There are two species of *Chamerion* in Idaho. This genus was formerly known as *Epilobium*.

Use: Leaves and tender portions are edible.

Range: Somewhat widespread

Similarity to toxic species: Fireweed could be confused with other plants when not in flower, but when in flower, it cannot be confused with anything else.

Best time: Spring

Status: Common in certain areas, especially in burned or clear-cut areas. A known fire-follower.

Tools needed: Clippers to collect tender stems

Properties

As the common name implies, fireweed is a fire-follower, often sprouting up in large patches in areas that have recently burned. The species name *angustifolium* (narrow-leaved) is constructed from the Latin words *angustus*, for "narrow," and *folium*, for "leaf."

The reddish stems of this herbaceous perennial are usually erect, smooth, and rise 2 to nearly 8 feet tall. Alternately arranged leaves are lanceolate and more or less pinnately veined. The flowers have four magenta to pink petals, each 2 to 3 centimeters in diameter. The styles have four stigmas, and there are eight stamens.

The reddish-brown linear seed capsule splits from its apex. It bears hundreds of minute brown seeds, which blow about and spread the plant. Fireweed also spreads by its underground roots, and eventually forms a large patch.

The plant before it flowers. JEAN PAWEK

The flowering fireweed. SIMON TONGE

Uses

The very youngest shoots can be snapped off and boiled or steamed like asparagus. The young shoots were collected in the spring by various Native peoples and cooked alone or mixed with other greens, which you can do too.

As the plant matures, the leaves become tough and somewhat bitter, but could still be cooked to make them more palatable. The stems of the older plant can be peeled and eaten raw. Fireweed is a good source of vitamin C and vitamin A.

A tea made from the mature leaves has been used as a laxative. Blackfoot people crushed the root and made it into a poultice to treat various skin problems, like burns, cuts, and abrasions.

Various candies and jellies, and even ice cream, are made today in Alaska from the fireweed plant. Okay, so the jelly in the recipe that follows is not a "health food," but you might be able to tweak the recipe somehow and use a better sugar.

RECIPE

Fireweed Jelly

Gakona Baby of Alaska makes several batches of fireweed jelly each summer when the fireweed is in bloom. Gakona says that it is important that only the blooms be harvested, and not the stems. Also, she has tried this recipe with Certo and it does not set, so be sure to use Sure-Jell or a powdered pectin.

2½ cups fireweed juice (see below)

1 teaspoon lemon juice

½ teaspoon butter

1 (1¾ ounce) package dry pectin

3 cups sugar

Begin by making fireweed juice. Harvest about 8 packed cups of fireweed flowers, rinse thoroughly, and put in a 2-quart pot. Add just enough water so the water level is just below the top of the flowers. When finished, the juice should be a deep purple color—if it is brownish, too much water was used in the boiling process. Boil the flowers in water until the color is boiled out and the petals are a grayish color. Ladle the juice into a jar through cheesecloth to strain.

Warm the fireweed juice, lemon juice, and butter on the stovetop. Add the pectin, bring to a boil, and boil hard for 1 minute.

Add the sugar and bring to full boil for 1 minute. Skim the top of the jelly. Pour into a pitcher (making it easier to fill the jars) and skim again. Fill sterilized jars, leaving ⅛ inch of space at the top. Process in a hot water bath for 10 minutes.

Yields four 8-ounce jars.

—RECIPE FROM GAKONA BABY

EVENING PRIMROSE
Oenothera abucaulis, O. biennis, O. elata

There are 145 species of *Oenothera* recorded in North America, and fifteen of these are in Idaho.

Use: Roots for food; leaves for food and medicine
Range: Fields, dry land, gardens, farms
Similarity to toxic species: The young leaves can resemble young foxglove leaves. Make sure you know the difference before collecting.
Best time: Spring
Status: Somewhat common
Tools needed: Digging stick

Properties
Different species of *Oenothera* can be annual, biennial, or perennial. *O. biennis* can be found in vacant lots, open fields, along river banks, and in well-drained soils up to about the 2,000-foot level.

The flowers and leaf of the evening primrose. BARBARA EISENSTEIN

The flower of *Oenothera pallida*. BARBARA EISENSTEIN

This is an erect biennial with alternate leaves. When the plant first emerges, you will observe the basal rosettes of elliptical leaves. The lower leaves are stalked, whereas the upper leaves are sessile, or stalk-less, as the plants gets taller.

The fragrant flower is composed of four yellow petals, four sepals, and eight stamens. Each stamen supports a four-lobed stigma, which is the pollen-bearing part of the stamen. A narrow fruit follows the flowers, which is a four-celled capsule about 2 inches long.

Uses

The roots of the first year are generally sought for food. Dig the youngest roots, and then peel and cook them by boiling or by cooking in an underground pit. Younger roots are best, as the older ones get tough and strongly flavored. Sometimes, a change of water is required to make the roots palatable.

Slice the roots, and sauté or cook in stews. Boil them first if the roots are tough. Serve with butter or cheese.

Is this a really good food, or is it marginal? I think it depends on how hungry you are, and the age of the root. Older roots are simply not as tender or tasty as the young ones.

We've tried some leaves too—both raw and cooked—and they get mixed reviews. The young ones are okay when used sparingly in salads, but you're most likely to enjoy them a bit better when steamed or boiled, and blended with other foods.

The astringency of the leaves makes it useful for coughs and sore throats, either made into an infusion, or simply chewed.

LOPSEED FAMILY (PHRYMACEAE)

The Lopseed family contains fifteen genera worldwide, with 230 species. In Idaho, there are four genera of this family.

YELLOW MONKEY FLOWER

Erythranthe guttata (formerly *Mimulus guttatus*. The genus Mimulus had formerly been classified within the Figwort family.)

This group is currently undergoing revision as botanists are carefully examining it. Formerly *Mimulus*, there are twenty-seven identified species of *Erythranthe* in Idaho.

Use: Everything tender above the waterline is edible.

Range: Found in slow-moving waters or ponds, up to timberline

Similarity to toxic species: None

Best time: Spring

Status: Common in some areas; not particularly widespread

Tools needed: None

Monkey flower in bloom. HELEN W. NYERGES

Properties

This is a common yellow wild-flower that grows along the shallow banks of streams, in much the same environment as watercress. It's usually very conspicuous when in flower and fairly easy to recognize.

The bright yellow flowers are typically on a raceme, with five or so flowers per stalk. The flower is composed of an upper lip with two lobes and a lower lip with three lobes, which also may have many red to brown spots or just one large spot. The opening to the tubular flower is hairy. The leaves are opposite, round to oval in shape, usually with irregular teeth.

The plant may be an annual or perennial, with the stems either erect or sprawling in the water. It's a highly variable plant.

Another blooming monkey flower.

Uses

Since the yellow monkey flower grows in slow-moving waters, make sure that the water is clean if you plan to use it in salads.

I've used the leaves and tender stems in salads many times, and I just pinch off the tender above-water sections. The texture is good and the flavor is mild to bland, so it makes a good addition to salads, either alone or mixed with a variety of other wild greens for a balanced flavor. Add some tomatoes and avocado too. Of course, I nearly always add salad dressing to make it tasty, and the salad will have the flavor of whatever salad dressing you use.

The greens also lend themselves well to various cooked dishes. You can simply boil them like spinach, or you can try stir-frying with other greens and vegetables. Yellow monkey flower is mild and can always go into any soup or stew pot.

Caution

A couple of monkey flower species are endangered including *Erythranthe michiganesis* and *E. guttatus*.

PLANTAIN FAMILY (PLANTAGINACEAE)

The Plantain family has 110 genera and approximately 2,000 species worldwide. There are twenty-one genera found in Idaho.

PLANTAIN
Plantago major, P. lanceolata

There are about 250 species of *Plantago* worldwide, with eleven found in Idaho.

Use: Young leaves used for food; seeds used for food and medicine
Range: Prefers lawns, fields, and wet areas
Similarity to toxic species: None
Best time: Spring for the leaves; late summer for the seeds
Status: Fairly common
Tools needed: None

Properties
Plantain is as common an urban weed as dandelion, though not as widely known. It's usually found in lawns and fields, but also in wet areas.

All the leaves radiate from the base in a rosette fashion, with the basal leaves typically from about 2 to 6 inches in length. *P. lanceolata*'s leaves are narrow, prominently ribbed with parallel veins. *P. major* has broad, glabrous leaves, up to 6 inches long, roundish or ovate-shaped. Both have leaves covered with soft short hairs.

Broadleaf plantain going to seed. RICK ADAMS

Broadleaf plantain.

View of broadleaf plantain.

Roman examines a broadleaf plantain in the field.

Narrowleaf plantain.

The flowers are formed in spikes (somewhat resembling a miniature cattail flower spike), usually just a few inches long, and on stems that are typically no more than a foot tall. Each greenish flower is composed of four sepals, a small corolla, and four stamens (sometimes two). The flowers are covered by dry, scarious bracts. When the spikes are dry, you can strip off the seeds and winnow them.

Uses

The young tender leaves of spring are the best to eat; use in salads or as you would spinach. The leaves that have become more fibrous with age need longer cooking, and they are best finely chopped or pureed and cooked in a cream sauce. The leaves have a mild laxative effect.

The seeds can be eaten once cleaned by winnowing. They can be ground into flour and used as you would regular flour, or soaked in water (to soften) and then cooked like rice. Once cooked, the seeds are slightly mucilaginous and bland. They can be eaten plain or flavored with honey, butter, or other seasoning.

Plantain is a vulnerary plant (it promotes healing), and is noted for its styptic, antiseptic, and astringent qualities. Native people used the cooked leaves as a poultice for wounds. Cooked plantain leaves have been used as a direct poultice

View of narrow-leaf plantain.

on boils. Plantain leaf, crushed or chopped and used as a poultice, is perhaps the best herb to use for puncture wounds to the body (knife wound, stepping on a nail, etc.). Early American colonists used plantain on insect and venomous reptile bites, and used the seeds for expelling worms.

VERONICA (SPEEDWELL)
Veronica americana

The *Veronica* genus has about 250 species worldwide, nineteen of which are found in Idaho.

Use: The entire plant (tender stems and leaves) above the root can be eaten.
Range: Grows in slow-moving waters, in the same environment as watercress
Similarity to toxic species: None
Best time: Spring and summer
Status: Somewhat common
Tools needed: None

Veronica in a bed of watercress.

Properties

Veronica americana is a native, and has been confused with watercress because they both grow in water. The resemblance is superficial because there really are some obvious differences. The *Veronica* has a simple leaf about 1 or 2 inches long, whereas the watercress has pinnately divided leaves very much like many of the members of the mustard family. Watercress has a typical mustard flower formula, with four petals arranged like a cross, and its color is white. But the *Veronica* flower is lavender and asymmetrical with four petals, the upper one being wider than the others.

Veronica flower. RICK ADAMS

Uses

If I have no concerns about the safety of the water from which I've picked the veronica, I add it to salads. It is not strongly flavored, and you can use the entire plant. Just pinch it off at water level (no need to uproot the plant), rinse it, and then dice it into your salad. No need to pick off just the leaves—eat the entire above-water plant. Since it's so bland, you can mix it with stronger-flavored greens in your salad. It goes well with watercress, as well as any of the mustards.

View of the *Veronica* plant.

Veronica also goes well with soup dishes and stir-fries. It never gets strongly bitter, like watercress, and it never really gets fibrous. It's a mild plant that's fairly widespread in waterways.

If you live near a waterway where *Veronica* grows, you'll find it's a good plant to use in a variety of dishes where you might otherwise include spinach. Try some gently sautéed with green onions, and add some eggs to make an omelet. Try a cream soup into which you've gently cooked some *Veronica* greens.

BUCKWHEAT FAMILY (POLYGONACEAE)

The Buckwheat family has forty-eight genera and about 1,200 species world-wide. Fourteen of these genera are found in Idaho.

AMERICAN BISTORT
Bistorta bistortoides

The genus *Bistorta* includes three species in Idaho. This plant was formerly referred to as *Polygonum bistortoides*.

American bistort. MATT BELOW

Use: Edible leaf, root, and seed
Range: Moist meadows and forest clearings, from the foothills to above timberline
Similarity to toxic species: When not in flower, this could easily be confused for another, possibly toxic, plant.
Best time: Leaves and roots in spring; seeds in late summer
Status: Common
Tools needed: Trowel

Properties

American bistort are perennial herbs with stems rising from 2 to 8 feet tall. The leaves have long stalks, with the blade up to 6 inches long. Most of the leaves are basal, and the leaves that appear on the flower stalks are shorter and thinner. The leaves are elliptic to lanceolate-oblong. The rhizomes are contorted.

Uses

All members of *Bistorta* are edible, though palatability varies. The root of *B. bistortoides* can be eaten raw or cooked (boiled, baked, roasted). The flavor is somewhat like a chestnut.

The seeds—as with all the members of this genus and family—can be used for food. They are generally best winnowed and ground, and then cooked into a hot mush or some sort of bread or biscuit.

The leaves are also okay to eat, though you should use only the very young leaves for salads. The leaves can also be steamed or boiled and served like spinach, or added to soups, stews, egg and rice dishes, etc.

Lewis and Clark

In the journals of the Lewis and Clark expedition, the explorers found and described American bistort "in moist grounds on the quamash flats." They do not say whether they ate any.

MOUNTAIN SORREL
Oxyria dignya

There are four species of *Oxyria*, and apparently only this species is found in Idaho.

Use: Edible leaves and seeds
Range: Found at higher elevations
Similarity to toxic species: None
Best time: Spring and summer
Status: Sporadic
Tools needed: A collection bag

Properties

This plant seems to prefer the harsher environment of higher elevations, never growing in massive stands, but a little here, a little there. It's relatively easy to recognize and collect a few leaves for your meal.

This is a perennial herb with mostly basal leaves. The leaves are heart-shaped to kidney-shaped, about 2 inches across and on a stem that's about 3 to 4 inches long. The erect stem rises no more than 8 to 10 inches tall.

If you're familiar with the other members of this family, like dock or sheep sorrel, you'll probably notice the family resemblance. The flowers are also typical of this family, with many green to reddish flowers clustered on the stalk, which rises about a foot tall. There are four perianth segments, with the outer two spreading. There are six stamens and two red

Close-up of mountain sorrel seed. STEVE MATSON

The mountain sorrel plant.
BARBARA EISENSTEIN

stigmas. When the seeds mature in the fall, they will be more conspicuously red, flat, and winged like the dock seeds.

Uses

Mostly found in the higher elevations, this isn't a backyard plant. You might add some to a meal when out hiking or backpacking.

The leaves are tart, like sheep sorrel, and are great added to salads. Try them with an avocado salad. They're also good in a mixed salad. The leaves are a great addition to stews, soups, freeze-dried meals, MREs, etc. The flavor is very much like oxalis or sour grass, so you'll be adding this to other recipes, not making dishes from it entirely. A handful of the leaves makes a tart addition to soups cooked up on the trail.

SHEEP SORREL
Rumex acetosella

There are about 190 to 200 species of *Rumex* worldwide, with at least seventeen in Idaho, not counting varieties or subvarieties.

Use: The leaves are good raw in salads and can also be added to various cooked dishes.
Range: Found at higher elevations, often around water, and often near disturbed soils and in urban areas
Similarity to toxic species: None
Best time: Spring to early summer
Status: Can be abundant locally
Tools needed: None

Properties
Sheep sorrel is native to Europe and Asia. It is common and widespread, and is recognized by its characteristic leaves, which are generally basal, lance- to oblong-shaped, with the base tapered to hastate or sagittate. In other words, it looks like an elongated arrowhead. When the seed stalk matures, it is brown, reminiscent of the curly dock seed stalk but much smaller.

Sheep sorrel. GARY GONZALES

View of the sheep sorrel plant.

Uses

Where the plant is common, you can pinch off many of the small leaves to add to salad, or even to use as the main salad ingredient. I've enjoyed sheep sorrel salads with just avocado and dressing added. The leaves are mildly sour, making a very tangy salad.

Sheep sorrel.
LOUIS-M. LANDRY

The flavor is somewhat similar to the leaves of oxalis, though not as strong. They can be effectively added raw to other foods like tostadas (in place of lettuce) or sandwiches. They add a bit of a tang when added to soups and stews, and can be very effective at livening up MREs.

RECIPE

Shiyo's Garden Salad

Rinse a bowl full of young sheep sorrel leaves. Add at least 1 ripe avocado and 1 ripe tomato, both diced. Toss with some Dr. Bronner's oil and vinegar dressing. Eat it outside where the wind can blow your hair.

CURLY DOCK
Rumex crispus

BROAD-LEAFED DOCK
Rumex obtusifolius

There are about 190 to 200 species of *Rumex* worldwide, with at least seventeen in Idaho, not counting varieties or subvarieties.

Use: Young dock leaves eaten raw or cooked; seeds harvested and added to various flours; stems used like rhubarb
Range: Prefers wet areas, but can be found in most environments
Similarity to toxic species: None
Best time: The leaves are best gathered when young in the spring. The seeds mature in late August, and they may be available for months.
Status: Common and widespread
Tools needed: None

Properties
Curly dock is a widespread, perennial, invasive plant in Idaho. It is originally from Europe, and today is not only found in Idaho, but worldwide. Though it has many good uses, it is often despised and poisoned because it not only survives well, but often takes over entire areas.

Christopher next to a dock patch. RICK ADAMS

The root looks like an orange carrot, and the spring leaves arise directly from the root. The young leaves are long and linear, and curved on their margins. The leaves can be over a foot long and pointed.

As the season progresses, the flower stalk arises, and it can reach about 4 feet, even taller in ideal conditions. The seeds are formed with three to each unit, with a papery sheath around the seed. They are green at first and then mature to a beautiful chocolate brown.

Uses

You can make meals from both the leaves and the mature seeds of curly dock. Let's start with the leaves.

Pick only the very youngest leaves for salad—the smaller ones before the plant has begun to send up its seed stalk. These will be not too tough and the flavor will be sour, somewhat like French sorrel. You can just rinse them, dice them, and add them to salads. I've had *only* these for salad, with dressing and avocado, and it was good, but only because the leaves were young.

Older leaves are best boiled like spinach, or—ideally with the midrib removed—sautéed with potatoes and onions. Or you can just add some to soups and stews. The leaves change color and darken a bit upon cooking, and the cooking softens them up. But you really want to cook older leaves, as

William Hartman (of Brier, Washington) in a patch of curly dock.

Young dock, ideal for cooking or salads.

Dock leaves, not too young, not too old, some for salad, some for soup. RICK ADAMS

they are tougher and bitter and astringent, all of which is reduced somewhat by cooking.

I have seen the brown seed spikes sold in floral supply shops as "fall decoration," and they are very attractive. Those little seeds can be stripped off the stalks with your hands, and then rubbed between the hands to remove the wing from the seed. You don't have to be too picky here, as it can all be used. I blow off the wings and then mix the seed half-and-half with flour for pancakes, and sometimes add them to bread batter. You could also toss some seed into soup to increase the protein content.

I've seen some folks go to the trouble of winnowing and then further grinding the seeds in a mill to get a fine flour. I never bother, but some folks prefer the finer flour, which is a bit more versatile than the seeds. For example, a fine flour can be mixed half-and-half

The maturing seed stalks of dock.

with wheat, blended, and put through a pasta machine to make a curly dock seed pasta, which tastes really good.

The leaf stems are tart and sour, but often make a good nibble. Young stems can be processed and used like rhubarb for pies.

PURSLANE FAMILY (PORTULACACEAE)

The Purslane family has recently been redefined by botanists as having only the one genus, with about one hundred species worldwide, and only this species is found in Idaho. Many of the plants that were formerly in this family are now a part of the Miner's Lettuce family. This family was considered by Dr. Leonid Enari to be entirely safe for consumption.

PURSLANE
Portulaca oleraceae

Use: The entire aboveground plant can be eaten raw, cooked, pickled, etc.
Range: Prefers disturbed soils of gardens and rose beds; also found in sandy areas around rivers
Similarity to toxic species: Somewhat resembles prostrate spurge. However, spurge lacks the succulence of purslane. Also, when you break the stem of spurge, a white milky sap appears.
Best time: Spring into summer
Status: Relatively common
Tools needed: None

The sprawling purslane plant.

Properties

Purslane starts appearing a bit later than most of the spring greens, typically by June or July. It is a very common annual in rose beds and gardens, though I do see it in the wild occasionally, typically in the sandy bottoms around streams.

The stems are succulent, red-colored, and round in the cross section. The stems sprawl outward from the roots, rosette-like, just lying on the ground. The leaves are paddle shaped. The little yellow flower is five-petaled.

Young purslane.

Uses

When you chew on a fresh stem or leaf of purslane, you'll find it mildly sour and a bit crunchy. It's really a great snack, though I like it a lot in salads. Just rinse to get all the dirt off, dice, add some dressing, and serve. Yes, add tomatoes and avocado, if you have any.

A patch of purslane.

Add purslane to sandwiches, tostadas, even to the edges of your chile rellenos and huevos rancheros. I've also eaten it fried, boiled, baked (in egg dishes), and probably other ways too. It's versatile, tasty, and crisp. It really goes with anything, and it's very nutritious.

If you take the thick stems, clean off the leaves, and cut them into sections of about 4 inches, you can make purslane pickles. There are many ways to make pickles; my way is to simply fill a jar with purslane stems, add raw apple cider vinegar, and let it sit for a few weeks. (I refrigerate it.)

According to researchers, purslane is one of the richest plant sources of omega-3 fatty acids. That means not only is it good, it's good for you.

RECIPE

Purslane Salsa

2 cups chopped tomatoes

2½ cups chopped foraged purslane

¾ cup chopped onions

3 garlic cloves

1 cup apple cider vinegar

¼ cup sugar

1 large Oregon myrtle leaf

½ cup chopped cilantro and some herbs from the garden (thyme, etc.)

Salt and pepper to taste

Place all the ingredients except the cilantro, herbs, and salt and pepper in a pot, bring to a boil, and then simmer until the right consistency (light or chunky). Add the cilantro and herbs at the end, and salt and pepper to taste.

Pour into jars, close the lids, and place in the fridge. It should be good for at least a month.

—RECIPE FROM PASCAL BAUDAR

PRIMROSE FAMILY (PRIMULACEAE)

There are twenty-five genera in this family, with about 600 species worldwide. In Idaho, we find six of those genera.

SHOOTING STAR
Dodecatheon spp.

There are about fourteen species of *Dodecatheon,* with eight found in Idaho (not counting varieties).

Use: All tender portions edible
Range: Prefers wet soils
Similarity to toxic species: None
Best time: March to May
Status: Widespread
Tools needed: A collection bag, possibly a trowel

Properties

These perennials herbs are distinctive plants, with flowers appearing on leafless stems. The flower stems are covered with fine hairs. The simple oval leaves are all basal, with short petioles. The margin of the leaf is lined with fine teeth.

The flower is bright pink, typically with a bit of yellow at the base of each petal. Each flower is about an inch long, with the petals sweeping back, giving the impression of a shooting star usually nodding downward. The dark purple anthers project forward and downward.

Each plant usually grows about 8 inches tall, with from one to five flowers per plant. Some, however, can grow over a foot tall and produce a few dozen flowers. The difference is usually a factor of the environment and availability of water.

It's a very distinctive plant that is hard to confuse with anything else.

A view of the shooting star flower.
BARBARA EISENSTEIN

Uses

If you taste a single leaf raw, you will probably enjoy the flavor but find the leaf texture a bit tough. Cooking improves the texture, and mellows the flavor. These are easily added to cooked dishes, and the easiest would be soups and stews.

The leaves of the shooting star plant. LILY JANE TSONG

Yes, even the flowers can be eaten. The flavor is good, though not exceptional. Still, these add some striking color to your camp salads, and will definitely spice up the conversation.

The roots are said to also be edible, once roasted or boiled. The few that I examined seemed to be small, and hardly worth the work for a nibble on the side. Plus, you're killing the plant to uproot it for such a small addition to your meal. I suggest that you enjoy the flower, and just sample a few leaves without uprooting the plant.

ROSE FAMILY (ROSACEAE)

The Rose family contains 110 genera and 3,000 species worldwide. At least forty-three of these genera are found in Idaho.

SERVICEBERRY (SASKATOON; JUNEBERRY)
Amelanchier alnifolia, A. pallida, A. utahensis

The *Amelanchier* genus consists of about twenty-five species, found all over North America. At least four are found in Idaho.

Use: Edible berries
Range: Most common in riparian and moist hillside areas, all the way up to alpine areas
Similarity to toxic species: None
Best time: Late summer and fall
Status: Somewhat common
Tools needed: Collecting basket

Properties

Serviceberry is a large shrub or small tree with deciduous leaves, often forming in dense thickets. There are at least three recorded varieties of *A. alnifolia*.

The twigs of this native are glabrous, and the leaf is elliptical to round, with obvious serrations, generally serrated above the middle of the leaf. The flowers are

Serviceberry and fruit. JOHN DOYEN

five-petaled, white, fragrant, and in clusters of a few to many. The fruit is a pome of two to five papery segments, berry-like, generally spherical, bluish-black to purple in color, with a waxy outer skin. Each fruit contains two seeds. The shape somewhat resembles a tiny pomegranate.

Uses

The ripe fruits are good to eat raw, dried, or prepared into jams, etc. Fruits of several species of *Amelanchier* were used for food by various Native American tribes, and all members of this genus are edible. Fruits ripen in late spring and into the summer.

A view of the ripe fruit. LOUIS-M. LANDRY

Native peoples ate these fruits fresh, or they dried them for later use. The ripe berries were mashed with water into a paste by some western indigenous people and then eaten fresh. Several of the western tribes were known to dry these fruits and then shape them into loaves for future use.

The berries remain sweet when dried, and could be reconstituted later when added to water. In some cases, this would be served as a sweet soup. With sugar and flour added, these fruits have been made into a pudding. The fruit can be dried, ground, and used in a pemmican mix.

HAWTHORN
Crataegus spp.

There are about 300 species of *Crataegus* worldwide. There are ten species in Idaho, including *C. chrysocarpa, C. douglasii, C. gaylussacia, C. macracantha, C. monogyna,* and *C. rivularis.*

Use: Fruit edible
Range: Widespread, but prefers riparian thickets
Similarity to toxic species: None
Best time: Late summer
Status: Common
Tools needed: A basket

Properties
This is a deciduous tree, or large shrub, found widespread throughout the Western states from Canada to California. The leaves are ovate, alternately arranged, with teeth that all point upward to the tip of the leaf. Its white to pink flowers are about ¼ inch across, forming flat terminal clusters. Each urn-shaped flower has five petals, and many stamens. When fully in flower, there is a strong flavor, often described as unpleasant. The red to black fruits are in clusters, with each fruit having two to five seeds. The plant is covered with 1- to 3-inch thorns along the branches.

Uses
The ripe berries are pleasant-flavored, though they are only mildly sweet, seedy, and somewhat dry. Well worth consuming fresh when encountered, the abundant hard seeds make processing and storage tricky. The pectin-rich pulp, squeezed through cloth or your fingers, will make a mild-flavored fruit leather. Alternately, commercial strainers can be used. The fruits have heart-supporting properties and help prepare the metabolism for winter.

The fruit was eaten fresh by many of the tribes that lived in the High Plains through and beyond Idaho. The fruits were used fresh, but also dried (often mashed into cakes) and stored for future use. Sometimes the fruits were soaked in water and made into a drink. Fruits were also mixed into pemmican mixes, which was typically a mix of dried and crumbled meats, and suet.

Among some tribes, these berries were only used sparingly, or regarded as "famine food," when nothing more desirable was available.

The ripe hawthorn fruit. KYLE CHAMBERLAIN

Cautions

Consume the fruits with caution and moderation the first time you try them, as some users have reported stomachaches after consuming these. The fruit contains cardiac glycosides. It may interfere with a heart patient's medications, perhaps potentiating or inhibiting. It is considered hypotensive and may lower blood pressure.

STRAWBERRY
Fragaria spp.

Fragaria contains twenty species worldwide, with four found wild in Idaho, not including varieties or subspecies.

Use: Edible berries; leaves used for tea
Range: Can be found from lower elevations up the mountain meadows
Similarity to toxic species: None
Best time: Spring and summer
Status: Widespread
Tools needed: Collecting basket

Properties
If you've grown strawberries in your yard, you will recognize these two wild strawberries:

The wood strawberry (*F. vesca*) is found in partial shade in the forests throughout Idaho. The receptacle is about 5 to 10 millimeters; the leaf petiole is generally 3 to 25 centimeters.

Ground cover of wild strawberry.

Fruit of *F. vesca.* DR. AMADEJ TRNKOCZY

The mountain strawberry (*F. virginiana*) is found in the higher elevations in meadows and forest clearings. The receptacle is more or less about 10 millimeters; the leaf petiole is generally 1 to 25 centimeters.

The leaves of both strawberries are all basal, generally three-lobed, with each leaflet having fine teeth. They look just like the strawberries you grow in your garden, but smaller.

Technically, the strawberry berry is an aggregate accessory fruit, meaning that the fleshy part is derived not from the plant's ovaries but from the receptacle that holds the ovaries. In other words, what we call the "fruit" (because, obviously, it looks like a fruit) is the receptacle, and all the little seeds on the outside of the "fruit" are technically referred to as achenes, actually the ovaries of the flower, with a seed inside it.

Though the wild strawberry prefers forests and clearings at higher elevations, it is found widely throughout the state.

FORAGER NOTE: Strawberry leaf tea (made by infusion), though not strongly flavored, is popular in many circles. It is high in vitamin C and generally used as you'd use blackberry leaf or raspberry leaf tea. It's a mild diuretic and has astringent properties, and is regarded as a tonic for the female reproductive system. When made stronger, the tea is said to be good for hay fever.

Wild strawberry flowers and leaves (*F. vesca*). JEAN PAWEK

Wild strawberries are pretty easy to identify. When the average person sees one, especially if it's summer and the plant is in fruit, he or she will typically say, "Hey, look, isn't that a wild strawberry?" Strawberries are so widely known that just about everyone recognizes them when they see them, even though the wild varieties are significantly smaller than the huge ones that can be found in markets. Cultivated strawberries can get to be about 2—even up to 3—inches long. That's huge! By contrast, a wild strawberry is between ¼- and ½-inch long. A ½-inch wild strawberry is a big one!

Though they may be smaller, the wild strawberries are typically sweeter, firmer, and tastier than cultivated varieties. Yes, it may take longer to collect them, but you'll find that it's worth it.

Uses

You use wild strawberries in every way that you'd use cultivated strawberries. Eat them as is, dry them, make them into jams and jellies, put them on top of ice cream and pancakes, etc.

From Alaska and throughout the West, wherever strawberries grow, nearly all native peoples ate these fruit. Typically, these were eaten fresh. The berries of the beach (or sand) strawberry were eaten by all the Native people.

APPLE
Malus pumila, Malus hybrids

Worldwide, there are about twenty-five species of the *Malus* genus, which includes all of our domestic apples. In Idaho, we find at least four species of *Malus*, including *M. pumila* (the domestic apple and its varieties), and the crab apple (*M. hybrids*).

Use: Edible fruits
Range: Occurring in Alaska south to California. Found in moist woods, swamps, and open canyons from sea level to moderate elevations in the mountains.
Similarity to toxic species: None
Best time: Fall through winter
Status: Common
Tools needed: Collecting basket

Properties

If you've ever seen a domestic apple tree in an orchard or backyard, you know what the tree looks like. In the wild, these will be small trees, often in thickets. You'll look at the leaves, and the fruit, and you'll say to yourself, "Boy, that sure looks like an apple." Yes, it is an apple, a wild apple.

Each leaf is lanceolate to ovate-lanceolate, 4 to 10 centimeters long, pointed, serrate, occasionally with a lobe on one or both margins. It is deep green above, paler beneath.

The floral inflorescence typically has five to twelve flowers, and is flat-topped. There are five white petals; twenty stamens, shorter than the petals; and usually three styles.

The fruits are fleshy, round to obovoid, about 10 to 16 millimeters long. The color can range from yellow to purplish-red.

Uses

Remember, if you know what an apple looks like, you'll recognize the crab apples or crabbies. Probably everyone who has seen one for the first time has picked one, chewed on it, and spit it out because it was too sour. These are not great to eat raw, like you'd eat

A view of the wild crab apple in fruit. WILLIAM J. HARTMAN

Wild crabapples. JEAN PAWEK

A wild crab apple. ZOYA AKULOVA

a regular domestic apple. But they are still a great find. The first time I saw a crab apple tree was when I was away from home visiting my cousin. We were in an area where the crab apples grew thickly, and I picked one for the first time, recognizing that it was an apple. I bit into it, and thought it was good. "We don't eat those," said my cousin disdainfully. "They give you the runs."

In fact, properly prepared, these can be quite good. I've cooked them, and run them through a sieve to get rid of the seeds and skin, and made a great crab apple sauce. You can sweeten with a bit of honey, as you wish.

The fruits can be dried as a snack for later, or mashed and added to other baked goods. The fruits can be cooked, mashed, strained, and used as the basis for an apple drink. The cooking mellows the flavor but you still might want to add some honey, and this goes particularly well with a cinnamon stick.

You can pretty much do anything with crab apples that you'd do with cultivated apples, such as cooking and mashing up a batch, spreading it thin in a pan and drying it for fruit leather. If you're good in the kitchen, you can cook up a batch of the small crab apples to make jams or jellies.

The fruits often remain in the trees and will lose a bit of their tartness and even sweeten up a bit if you harvest in the winter time.

You might be surprised how many gone-feral apple trees you can find that still produce fruit. Some of the best apples I've ever eaten were picked in orchards that had been abandoned at least a decade earlier, yet they still consistently produced quality fruit.

Cautions

The seeds of crab apples and domestic apples are toxic because of a small amount of a cyanide compound. But you'd have to eat many apples to cause sickness, and if you don't chew the seeds, they will just pass through your body. An adult could die if he or she chewed up about a half-cup of pure seed at one sitting. Fortunately, cooking and drying help to break down this chemical, significantly reducing any danger.

WILD CHERRIES AND STONE FRUITS
Prunus spp.

There are about 400 species of *Prunus* worldwide, whose common names generally include cherry, almond, apricot, and plum. At least nineteen species of *Prunus* are recorded in Idaho.

Use: Flesh of the fruit used in jams and jellies; meat of the large seed processed into a flour
Range: Canyons, lowland forests, hillsides, farmland, urban areas
Similarity to toxic species: In a sense, this is a toxic plant. The leaves are mildly toxic—see the Cautions below.
Best time: Fruits mature from July into August.
Status: Common
Tools needed: None

Properties
One way to identify the plant is to crush the leaves, wait a few seconds, and then smell them. They will have a distinct aroma of bitter almond extract, your clue that the leaf contains "cyanide" (hydrocyanic acid).

The fruits are very much like cultivated cherries, except the color is darker red, almost maroon, sometimes even darker. The flesh layer can be very thin in

A wild cherry leaf. LOUIS-M. LANDRY

The fruit of wild cherry. LOUIS-M. LANDRY

Chokecherry *Prunus Virginiana.* BOB KRUMM

Chokecherry blossoms. BOB KRUMM

dry years, and thicker in seasons following good rains. Like domestic cherries, there is a thin shell and the meaty inside of the seed.

Wild cherries and plums (*Prunus avium, P. cerasifera, P. spinosa,* and *P. domestica*) are widespread in lowlands. *P. armeniacia* can occur in the bunchgrass zone. *P. dulcis* is known to naturalize in the hottest parts of the sagebrush zone. Here, we're primarily concerned with the cherries: chokecherry (*P. virginiana*), bitter cherry (*P. emarginata*), and western chokecherry (*P. virginiana var. demissa*).

Uses

The fruit of wild cherries makes a great trail nibble. I usually see them in August when they ripen, when the trail is hot and dry, and the fruit makes a refreshing treat, if not too sour. But don't eat too many of the raw fruit, or diarrhea might result.

The wild cherry also has a hint of bitterness. The fruit can be cooked off the seeds, and the pulp made into jellies, jams, and preserves. You can also make a fruit leather by laying the pulp on a cookie sheet and drying it.

In the old days, Native people enjoyed the flesh of the cherry, but they considered the seed to be the more valuable part of the fruit. The seeds were shelled and the inside meat was cooked to reduce the cyanide. The cooked seeds, once ground into mush or meal, were then used to make a sweet bread product or added (like acorns) to stews as a gravy or thickening agent.

The bark was boiled by Native people and used as a cough and sore throat remedy, as well as for treating diarrhea and headaches.

Cautions

If you crush the leaf, it will impart a sweet aroma like the bitter almond extract used in cooking. That's the telltale aroma of cyanide, so don't use the leaf for tea.

Eat a large volume, relative to your body size, and you could have stomach pains or diarrhea, so exercise caution.

Lewis and Clark

On June 11, 1805, Meriwether Lewis became sick and wrote, "I was taken with such violent pain in the intestens that I was unable to partake of the feast of marrowbones. . . . I directed a parsel of the small twigs [of chokecherry] to be geathered striped of their leaves, cut into pieces of about 2 Inches in length and boiled in water until a strong black decoction of an astringent bitter tast was produced; at sunset I took a point [pint] of this decoction and abut an hour after repeated the dze. By 10 in the evening I was entirely relieved from pain and in fact every symptom of the disorder forsook me; my fever abated, a gentle perspiration was produced and I had a comfortable and refreshing nights rest."

WILD ROSE
Rosa spp.

There are about one hundred species of *Rosa* worldwide, which hybridize freely. At least eleven species can be found in the wild in Idaho, not including varieties, and not including the large array of cultivated roses grown in gardens. The exotics include *R. canina, R. eglanteria,* and *R. multiflora.* The natives include *R. pisocarpa, R. gymnocarpa, R. nutkana, R. rugosa,* and *R. woodsii.* All species are widespread at low and middle elevations.

Use: Fruits eaten raw or cooked and made into jam or tea; wood useful for arrow shafts
Range: Typically riparian, but found in many areas; cultivated roses common in urban areas
Similarity to toxic species: None (but be wary of eating fruit or flower from roses where various commercial fertilizers and insecticides have been used).
Best time: Fruits mature in summer
Status: Common
Tools needed: Clippers, possibly gloves

Properties
Wild roses are more common than most people think. They are typically found in wet areas, though this is not a fast rule. The wild rose flowers are five-petaled, not

Wild rose hips.

the multiple-petal flowers that you find on hybridized roses. After the flowers mature and fade the fruit develops, often called the "hip," which is usually smaller than a grape. The fruit is bright orange.

The leaves are oddly divided into three, five, or seven petals, and the stalks are covered in thorns. If you've ever had rose bushes in your yard, you have a pretty good idea of what the wild rose looks like.

The wild rose is often in dense thickets. If it gets cut down, or after a burn, there will be many straight shoots in the new growth.

Wild rose flower.

Uses

For food, we have the flower and the fruits. The flowers have long been used to make "rosewater" and could also be used to make a mild-flavored infusion. The petals make a flavorful, colorful, and nutritious garnish for soups and salads.

The fruits—commonly called "hips"—are one of the richest sources of vitamin C. The fruits can be eaten fresh, but you should first split them open and scrape out the more fibrous insides. They are typically a bit fibrous, with a hint of bitterness. The fruits are more commonly cooked into a tea or made into jellies.

Some "old-school" archers consider the rose shaft one of the finest woods to use for making arrows, assuming you cut the new straight shoots. You need to then ream the shaft through a rock with a hole in it to remove the thorns.

Cautions

Before you eat the petals or fruit, make sure the plants have not been sprayed with any pesticides.

BLACKBERRY/BRAMBLES
Rubus spp.

There are 400 to 750 species of *Rubus* worldwide, including at least sixteen in Idaho (not including varieties). These include blackberry, raspberry, and salmonberry (aka thimbleberry; *R. parviflorus*).

Use: Berries used for juices, jams, and desserts, or dried; leaves used for medicine
Range: Riparian and many other areas where sufficient water is supplied
Similarity to toxic species: Somewhat resembles poison oak, though poison oak lacks the thorns
Best time: Fruits mature in summer
Status: Very common
Tools needed: None, but clippers can help

Properties
Even non-botanists can usually identify the vine and fruit of the very common blackberry. In some parts of Idaho, wild blackberries are so common that most go uneaten. They are sometimes regarded as a nuisance.

Blackberries in flower.

Rubus armeniacus fruit.

Fruiting blackberry.

The leaves are palmately divided (like a hand) into three, five, or seven segments. The vines are twining on the ground or over low hedges, and are characterized by their thorns, which makes it difficult to wade too deep into any of the old hedge-like stands of wild blackberries. The flowers are white, five-petaled, and followed by the fruits, which are aggregate.

Most people instantly recognize the shape of the blackberry because they've seen it in supermarkets or in backyard gardens. The aggregate fruit is a collection of sweet drupelets, with the fruit separating from the flower stalk to form a somewhat hollow, thimble-like shape.

Uses

The blackberry is fairly universally recognized, and everyone who sees the ripe ones ventures out to eat them. I've picked them in the foothills and mountains, and along roadsides. The key is to avoid the thorns, and to make sure they are not immature and tart. If the fruit is black, soft, and easily picked, it's ripe! You can eat the berries right away, or pick a bunch and mash them for a pancake, biscuit, or cake topping. Even better, sprinkle them over a bowl of vanilla ice cream. (Yes, we know that chocolate ice cream is better for you, but the flavor of blackberries clashes a bit with chocolate.)

You could also make a conserve, a jam, a jelly, a pie filling, or a juice. It's a very versatile berry. And though I rarely have ripe blackberries around long enough to dry them, they can be dried in any food dehydrator and will keep for quite a while. The dried fruits can then be eaten as is, or reconstituted for juices or deserts.

An infusion of the leaves has long been used among Native Americans for diarrhea and childbirth pains.

Lewis and Clark

Lewis and Clark collected a sample of thimbleberry near The Dalles, on the Columbia River in Oregon and Washington, on April 15, 1806. (The site was a major Native American trading center for at least 10,000 years.) Frederick Pursh described the sample as "a shrub of which the natives eat the young Sprout without kooking."

Salmonberry fruit. VERNON SMITH

A view of the thimbleberry plant. JEAN PAWEK

MOUNTAIN ASH
Sorbus spp.

There are about eighty species of *Sorbus.* In Idaho, we have five recorded species, including *S. aucuparia, S. scopulina,* and *S. sitchensis.*

Use: Fruits are eaten
Range: Mountain forests and around timberline
Similarity to toxic species: None
Best time: Summer and fall
Status: Common
Tools needed: A container for collecting

Properties
These are shrubs or small deciduous trees from 5 to 10 feet tall. The trees are most common on the edges of low to mid-elevation forests. The bark is reddish-brown to grey. The leaves are pinnate, with leaflets generally toothed. The leaflets are sharply serrated. The leaf is darker green on the top than below.

The small white flowers have five petals and five stamens, and are formed in clusters. The fruits are red to orange, and appear somewhat like little apples (to which they are related).

A view of the leaf and fruit. KYLE CHAMBERLAIN

A view of a mountain ash (*S. americana*). LOUIS-M. LANDRY

Uses

The fruits are a good source of vitamin C, and are often too tart to eat alone. After the first frost, the fruits are a bit more palatable. Sweetened with honey, and often mixed with other fruits, these are popular in juices, jams and jellies, and pie fillings. The berries can be soaked or cooked to reduce bitterness, and then mixed into cereals (hot or cold), or added to bread batter, or to tea. Some of Native peoples liked to add these fruits to soups, meat dishes, and fish dishes.

A view of the tree in fruit. JEAN PAWEK

A close-up of the mountain ash fruit.
LOUIS-M. LANDRY

Some people like these fruits, and some do not. According to Thomas Elpel, author of *Foraging the Mountain West*, "In my opinion, mountain ash fruits are wholly unpalatable, but some people like them."

According to William Schlegel, "I once offended a Blackfoot bus driver by talking about how I didn't think anyone would bother to eat these fruits any-more. He said that he did! He told me that he used them as a sauce for meat, much like you'd use cranberries."

Cautions

Avoid large amounts of the berries as they can cause stomach irritation and pain, vomiting, queasiness, diarrhea, kidney damage, and other side effects.

A view of the fruit.
JEAN PAWEK

SAXIFRAGE FAMILY (SAXIFRAGACEAE)

There are thirty-eight genera and about 600 species of the Saxifrage family worldwide. These occur mostly in Arctic and alpine territories, and some are cultivated. This family is undergoing much study, meaning that many of the former classifications are becoming obsolete. In Idaho, at least eighteen genera are represented, according to the latest thinking on this family.

BROOK SAXIFRAGE
Micranthes odontoloma, formerly *Saxifraga odontoloma, Saxifraga arguta*

There are approximately twenty species of *Micranthes* found in Idaho, and at least twelve species of *Saxifraga,* a closely related genus.

Note the round, neatly scalloped shape of the brook saxifrage plant. JEAN PAWEK

Use: Leaves are eaten.

Range: High mountain areas, typically along streams in alpine areas and wet meadows

Similarity to toxic species: None

Best time: Best collected spring into summer

Status: Widespread; found from southern Alaska south to California

Tools needed: A collection bag

Properties

This is a low-growing plant, rising no more than a foot or so tall, growing in clusters along the streams. It is an herbaceous perennial, with round to kidney-shaped leaves about 3 inches across. Each leaf blade arises from a

A view of the brook saxifrage plant. JEAN PAWEK

long stalk and is evenly toothed. The flower stalks arise up to about a foot and a half tall, with somewhat inconspicuous white to pink-toned flowers. Each flower consists of five separate, round, ephemeral petals, with five sepals, ten stamens, and one pistil.

In the higher mountain elevations, this is perhaps one of the most common plants you will see. It will be available when there is not much else available at that time or location.

Uses

The leaves make an excellent raw salad, especially when collected in the spring. The flavor is bland and the texture is ideal. They will take on the flavor of whatever you season them with, and you can add them to other greens that are more spicy or bitter to mellow them out. They are often available in abundance. While the young leaves alone make a good trail salad, they are better blended with other greens and ingredients for a mixed salad. The older leaves become a bit tough, and slightly bitter, and so should be cooked in soups or stews to tenderize.

According to wild food forager Tom Elpel, "Being nearly tasteless may not seem like a good marketing pitch for an edible wild plant, but in foraging, a lack of flavor is often the most desirable flavor of all. Gather a big bowl of this nearly tasteless salad, then toss in anything else for flavor: a few wild onions, some dandelion leaves, blue violets, aster blossoms, and maybe some clover and strawberry leaves. If you spend much time in the high country, you will quickly become a big fan of this little plant!"

NIGHTSHADE FAMILY (SOLANACEAE)

There are seventy-five genera of the Nightshade family and 3,000 species world-wide. Ten genera are found in Idaho. Many are toxic, and many are good foods.

BLACK NIGHTSHADE
Solanum nigrum, S. americanum

There are approximately 1,500 species of *Solanum* in the world, with twelve recorded in Idaho. *S. americanum* is a native, and *S. nigrum* is introduced. You are more likely to find *S. nigrum* in Idaho, and it's difficult to distinguish from *S. americanum*.

Use: Fruits eaten when ripe, raw, or cooked
Range: Disturbed soils; urban areas
Similarity to toxic species: According to many, this is a toxic species, meaning don't eat the raw green fruits, and don't eat the leaves raw. Sickness is possible in either case. There is also a slight resemblance to jimsonweed, which is in the same family.
Best time: Summer
Status: Somewhat common in weedy areas
Tools needed: None

Nightshade flower and immature fruit.

Properties

The very young plant much resembles lamb's-quarter, except that the nightshade doesn't have an erect stem. Rather, it's more widely branched. Also, though the individual leaves of both nightshade and lamb's-quarter are quite similar, the nightshade lacks the mealy coating of the lamb's-quarter and lacks the often noticeable red in the axil of the leaf that is common in lamb's-quarter.

The five-petaled white to lavender flower is a very typical nightshade family flower, resembling the flowers of garden tomatoes. The fruits begin as tiny, BB-size green fruits, and by August ripen into purplish-black little "tomatoes." We've eaten the listed *Solanums* with no problems.

Uses

The fruit of this plant seems to peak around August, when the plant can be prolifically in fruit if the season's rain and heat have been just right. Regardless, I have found ripe fruit of black nightshade during every month.

You don't want to eat these fruits raw while they are still green, as this could result in a stomachache and minor sickness. They should first be boiled, fried, or otherwise cooked. I will, on the other hand, try a few of the dark purple ripe fruits if I see them while hiking. I like the fresh tartness. It's very much like eating a tomato, but a bit spicier. They are great added to salads—just like adding tomatoes!

But just like tomatoes, there are many other ways to enjoy the ripe western nightshade fruit. We've smashed them and added them to pizza dough. They taste like potatoes, but turn nearly black when cooked. They are good added to

Ripe nightshade fruit.

soup too. You don't need to cut or slice them, since they are so small. Just toss them into your soup or stew.

Also, just like sun-dried tomatoes with their unique flavor, you can let western nightshade berries dry in the sun (or in your oven or food dryer) and then eat as is or reconstitute later into various recipes. Though it isn't absolutely necessary, I find that they dry quicker if you gently smash them first—such as on the cookie sheet that you'll be drying them on.

Cautions

While there are other ripe nightshade fruits that could be eaten, we don't advise you eat any but the one listed above. Also, do not eat the green berries. Only eat the fully ripe, dark purple berries. Otherwise, sickness could result. Green berries should only be consumed if boiled, fried, or otherwise cooked. Anyone with a tomato sensitivity, or sensitivity to other members of this family (e.g., eggplant, chilies, peppers), should not consume these fruits.

Nightshade fruit. DR. AMADEJ TRNKOCZY

ELM FAMILY (ULMACEAE)

Worldwide, there are about fifteen genera in the Elm Family; only the elms are found in Idaho.

SIBERIAN ELM TREE
Ulmus pumila

There are about twenty species of *Ulmus* worldwide, and one common in Idaho.

Use: Edible samaras (seeds)
Range: Throughout the entire United States
Similarity to toxic species: None
Best time: Mid to late spring; must observe the plant
Status: Invasive in some locations
Tools needed: A bag for collecting

Properties

The Siberian elm is a somewhat common, typically invasive tree that seems to sprout up of its own accord in diverse locations. Its preference is disturbed soils around farms and fields. You can find it along roadsides, in fields, and in washes.

Siberian elm leaves. MIKE KREBILL

Siberian elm samara (seeds). MIKE KREBILL

The bark is scaly and sheds regularly. The leaves are ovoid, about an inch to an inch-and-a-half in length. They are alternately arranged, pinnately veined, and serrated on their edges. The fruit is a winged nutlet, with the wings somewhat translucent. The clusters of the samaras—the winged seeds—form in the spring even before the leaves have appeared.

Uses

The young samaras can be collected, when tender, before they dry and fall. They are somewhat like a grain and somewhat like salad—and can be adapted to dishes for either. I have only eaten these fresh from the tree and found them to be mild, chewy, and good as a trail snack.

Other species of *Ulmus* do not appear to have been widely used for food by Native peoples. The wood, however, was often used for posts, wooden mortars, and various projects. The bark was used for some medicinal applications, and the inner bark from *Ulmus rubra* was actually cooked in animal fat and eaten as a snack.

Siberian elm samara (seeds).
MIKE KREBILL

NETTLE FAMILY (URTICACEAE)

The Nettle family includes fifty genera and 700 species worldwide. Two of these genera are found Idaho.

STINGING NETTLE
Urtica dioica; U. urens

Of the forty-five species of *Urtica* worldwide, only three (not counting subspecies) are found in Idaho.

Use: Leaves used for food and tea; stalks made into fiber

Range: Riparian, urban fields, edges of farms, disturbed soils, etc.

Similarity to toxic species: While nettle itself is regarded as a mechanical toxin by some botanists, it is safe to eat the cooked greens.

Best time: Collect the greens in the spring.

Status: Common

Tools needed: Gloves, snippers

Properties

This perennial generally sends up a single stalk in the winter or spring that can reach around 5 feet tall if undisturbed. The leaves are oblong, with toothed margins, and taper to a point. Both the leaves and the stalks are covered with bristles that cause a stinging irritation when you brush against them. Nettle can be found all over Idaho, along streams in the wilderness and in fields and backyards.

Note: There are three subspecies to *U. dioica.* The US Department of Agriculture plant website states that subspecies *dioica* is an introduced nettle (from

Young nettle plants.

Nettle leaves.

Gary Gonzales examines a tall nettle.

Europe originally), and the other two subspecies—*holosericea* and *gracilis*—are natives.

Uses

The young, tender leaf tips of nettle are the best to use, though you could also collect just the leaves later in the season (the stems get too tough). These tender tops can be steamed and boiled, which removes the sting of the nettles. They are tasty as a spinach-like dish, alone or served with butter or cheese or other topping. Also try the water from the boiling—it's delicious!

We've also made delicious stews and soups, which began by boiling the nettle tops. Then we quickly added diced potatoes, some red onions, and other greens. You can also add some miso powder. Cook until tender and then serve, perhaps with Bragg Liquid Aminos added for some great flavor and nutrition.

FORAGER NOTE: Nettles are an undervalued medicine, and herbalists speak highly of the many uses for nettle tea. I have found that drinking nettle tea in the spring helps to alleviate the symptoms of pollen allergies.

This is a vitamin-rich plant, so you'll be getting your medicine when you eat it.

Cautions

As you will probably learn from personal experience, you get "stung" when you brush up against nettle. This is due to the formic acid within each "needle," which causes a skin irritation. So be careful when you gather nettle greens by wearing gloves or other protection. And if you do get the nettle rash, you can treat it with fresh aloe vera gel or with the freshly crushed leaves of plants such as chickweed or curly dock.

RECIPE

Pascal's Stinging Nettle Hot Sauce

I created this hot sauce through experimentation and really enjoyed it. It has a mild "wild" flavor and was really liked by those who tasted it. It's extremely simple to make. This is a basic recipe, but you can add some of your favorite flavors and ingredients, such as Italian herbs, bay leaves, etc. As for supplies, you'll need latex gloves, a blender (or go primitive with a knife and a *molcajete*), jars or bottles, and a metal pot.

5 ounces jalapeño peppers, stemmed and chopped with seeds (make sure they're not too hot, though)

1 ounce serrano peppers

5 ounces fresh nettle leaves (or young nettles)

Juice from two limes

6 garlic cloves

3½ cups apple cider vinegar

1 teaspoon kosher or pickling salt

1 cup water or white wine (I used white wine in my original recipe)

Blend all the ingredients until smooth. Strain for a thinner sauce, or keep it as is for a thicker sauce. Transfer to jars and cover. Refrigerate at least 2 weeks, then enjoy!

—RECIPE FROM PASCAL BAUDAR

VIOLET FAMILY (VIOLACEAE)

There are twenty-three genera of this family and about 830 species, around 500 of which are *Viola*, the only genus found in Idaho.

VIOLET
Viola spp.

There are at least twenty-nine species of *Viola* recorded in Idaho, not including varieties.

Use: Edible leaves and flowers
Range: Widespread, growing in most environments in Idaho. You can find them in the prairies, foothills, urban areas, subalpine zones, etc.
Similarity to toxic species: None
Best time: Spring
Status: Common
Tools needed: A bag for collecting

Properties
Violets are commonly planted as garden plants, and they are hardy. They spread by their roots and appear to naturalize in areas where they were once cultivated. In fact, they are very easy to cultivate if you want some nearby for your meals.

Violets (*V. adunca*) in the wild. JEAN PAWEK

Wild *Viola odorata*. JEAN PAWEK

Though there is great variety in size and minor leaf characteristics, they all have heart-shaped leaves, usually on a long stem of a few inches. The flowers are white, purple, blue, and even yellow, though the cultivated ones are purple or blue.

Uses

When I learned you could eat violets, I began by collecting the heart-shaped leaves from neighbors' yards as I walked home from school. As I came to recognize them, I noticed that they were very common on the edges of people's yards, probably just going wild from an original planting. I'd pick a few leaves here and few there, and when I got home, I'd cook them up with a little water and season them with just butter. I loved them!

I have collected the tender leaves of spring, washed them and diced them, and added them to omelets. I've even tried some diced and added to ramen soup. They are very versatile, not strongly flavored, and can be added to many dishes.

The leaves are also edible raw, and add their mild flavor to salads. Some people find the leaves a bit strong or tough in salads, but it's really a matter of personal preference.

The flowers are often used to make jellies, or added to jellies, as well as used in various dessert items. I have had a gelatin product that someone else made using the purple flowers, and I thought it was very tasty. The edible flowers also add color to your salads.

Monocots

Monocot is short for "monocotyledon." When sprouted, these have one cotyledon, or embryonic leaf. Leaf veins are generally parallel from the base or midrib, and flower parts are generally in 3s. About half of all monocots are grasses. This group also include orchids, onions, lilies, and others.

WATER PLANTAIN FAMILY (ALISMATACEAE)

There are twelve genera worldwide of this family, with three genera found in Idaho. The *Alisma* genus, not treated here, is also an edible genus.

WAPATO
Sagittaria latifolia, S. cuneata

Of the twenty or so species of *Sagittaria*, at least five species have been spotted in Idaho. Many are easily recognized by their arrowhead leaves; others have lanceolate leaves. They always grow in permanent water.

Use: Bulbs are used raw or cooked, but mostly cooked.
Range: Considered a North American native, these have been found throughout Idaho in the lower wetland elevations, along slow streams, and at the edges of marshes and lakes.
Similarity to toxic species: There are some ornamental plants that bear a similarity to this arrowhead leaf.
Best time: Collect the tubers in the fall.
Status: Somewhat common
Tools needed: Possibly waders, or a canoe

The wapato flower. LOUIS-M. LANDRY

Properties

This plant is fairly easy to recognize, with its unmistakable arrowhead-shaped leaves, and because it always grows in swampy water or on the edges of lakes or slow streams. The little, white, three-petaled flowers are typically formed in whorls of three near the top of the naked stalk. The tubers are usually about the size of an egg, white-colored. A network of fine fibrous roots forms from the base of the leaves. The tubers will develop at various distances from the base of the leaves, usually a few feet away. The tubers are white with a smooth texture.

The arrowhead-shaped wapato leaf. LOUIS-M. LANDRY

Uses

The best time to harvest the tubers is late summer to fall, when they are largest. Once you have located a patch early in the year, you can go back later and collect where you see the dried wapato stalks. There seems to be no easy way to harvest these other than wading into the mud and separating the tubers from the fine roots with your feet.

I have tried simply pulling up the whole plant, and sometimes this works too. But usually I was only able to collect these by wading into the muddy water, loosening the tubers from the roots with my feet and toes, and then collecting them by hand. Some Native people were known to have collected the wapato tubers by going into the wet areas in a canoe, and pulling the plants up from the canoe.

Collect the bigger tubers and leave the rest. The tubers can average about an inch in diameter, and can be as small as a marble.

Once they are washed, you would use the tubers in any of the ways you might use potatoes: boiled, fried, baked. They are tasty, though the similarity to actual potatoes is slight. Though these can be eaten raw, they sometimes impart an irritation to the throat. To be safe, if you want to use as a salad food, boil first, chill, and then add other salad ingredients like tomatoes, hard-boiled eggs, dressing, etc.

This tuber was once an important staple for Northwestern Native peoples, including the Chinookan of the lower Columbia River, who gave the plant this name.

ONION (GARLIC) FAMILY (ALLIACEAE)

There are thirteen genera and 750 to 800 species of the Onion family worldwide. Some texts still refer to this group as part of Amaryllidaceae.

WILD ONIONS, ET AL.
Allium spp.

There are 750 to 800 species of *Allium* worldwide. These are found widely in North America, with at least twenty-six in Idaho. Most are natives. Some common ones include *Allium acuminatum, A. cernuum* (nodding onion), *A. douglasii, A. schoenoprasm,* and *A. validum.*

Use: Bulbs and greens eaten raw or cooked. However, I strongly advise the reader to leave the bulbs in the ground and only pick the greens for food.

Range: Can be found in just about every type of environment in Idaho

Similarity to toxic species: See Cautions.

Best time: The leaves and flowers are most noticeable in the spring and early summer.

Status: Though you will not find wild onions in certain areas, they can be common locally.

Tools needed: None

Field view of *A. biceptrum.* JEAN PAWEK

A view of *A. biceptrum*. JEAN PAWEK

A close view of *A. biceptrum*. JEAN PAWEK

Properties

Wild onions go by many names: ramps, wild garlic, leeks, etc. In general, they look like small "green onions" from the market, though many are inconspicuous when not in flower.

There is a small underground bulb, and the leaves are green and hollow. The flower stalk tends to be a bit more fibrous than the leaves. There appear to be six petals of the same color, but in fact there are three sepals underneath the three identical petals, giving the appearance of a six-petaled flower. The expedient field key to identifying a wild onion is the unmistakable aroma. If you don't have that aroma, you shouldn't use the plant because similar-appearing members of the Lily family could be toxic or poisonous.

Wild onions can be found all over the United States in a broad diversity of ecotypes. In Idaho, they are found throughout the valleys and in higher-elevation meadows and fields. We notice them mostly when they flower, because otherwise they appear very much like grass.

Uses

When you find wild onions, you'll be tempted to pull up the plant so you can eat the bulb. That's what you probably do in your own garden, but that's not the only way you can use these. Generally, I only pick the green leaves for consumption. If there are a lot of them, I might take some of the bulbs to eat, and break up the cluster and replant some. The reason I generally only eat the greens is that I've seen some patches of wild onions disappear entirely due to foragers uprooting the whole plant.

A view of *A. falcifolium.* JEAN PAWEK

A view of *A. hyalinum.* JEAN PAWEK

While the wild onion bulbs can be used in any of the myriad ways you're used to eating garlic, onions, chives, leeks, et al., you'll still get most of the flavor and most of the nutritional benefits by eating only the leaves. I pinch off a few leaves here, a few there, and add them to salads. Diced, they're great in soups, stews, egg dishes, and stir-fries. And, if you ever have to live off MREs, you can spice them up, and add to their nutritional value, by adding wild onion greens.

All tender parts of wild onions are edible, above- and belowground. Generally, the older flower stalks become fibrous and unpalatable. Otherwise, the bulbs and leaves are all used raw or cooked. Simply remove any outer fibrous layers of the plant, rinse, and then use in any of the ways you'd use green onions or chives.

Wild onions can be added to salads, used as the base for a soup, cooked alone as a "spinach," chopped and mixed into eggs, cooked as a side to fish, and used to enhance countless other recipes. Wild onions share many of the healthful benefits of garlic, and improve any urban or wilderness meal. Backpackers who are relying on dried trail rations will certainly enjoy the sustenance of wild onions. Many Native peoples heavily relied on wild onions and regarded them as a staple, not just a condiment.

Excellent health benefits are associated with eating any members of this group. Some of these benefits include lowering of cholesterol levels, prevention of flu, and reduction of high blood pressure. Used externally, the crushed green leaves can be applied directly to wounds to prevent infection.

A view of *A. validum.* JEAN PAWEK

Cautions

Never forget that some members of the Lily family with bulbs can be poisonous if eaten. Wild onions used to be classified in the Lily family because their characteristics are so similar. Make absolutely certain that you have correctly identified any wild onions that you intend to eat. You should check the floral characteristics to be certain that there are three sepals and three petals. Then, you must detect an obvious onion aroma. If there is no onion aroma, do not eat the plant. Though there are a few true onions that lack the onion aroma, it is imperative that you have absolutely identified those nonaromatic species as safe before you prepare them for food.

ASPARAGUS FAMILY (ASPARAGACEAE)

There are three genera in this relatively new family, created out of the Lily family (Liliaceae). Asparagaceae contains about 320 species, the majority of which (about 300) are a part of the *Asparagus* genus. There are twelve genera of this family in Idaho.

WILD ASPARAGUS
Asparagus officinalis

Of the approximately 300 species of *Asparagus*, this is the only one recorded in Idaho.

Use: Young shoots eaten
Range: Found in disturbed soils, valleys, and grasslands
Similarity to toxic species: See Cautions.
Best time: Spring
Status: Common in specific areas
Tools needed: Knife, bag

A bundle of asparagus spears.

Properties

The edible part of this European native are the first spring shoots, which are identical to the cultivated plant. Have you ever seen an asparagus spear in the produce section of your local grocery store or at a farmers' market? Now you know what wild asparagus looks like! Wild asparagus can be an escapee from gardens and farms, and would not be uncommon along a road or trail.

As the asparagus shoot continues to grow, numerous stems grow out of the main shoot. As these stems and their ferny leaves mature, the overall appearance of the plant begins to resemble a 3- to 5-foot-tall ferny bush. As the shoots grow, they become intricately branched, giving the entire plant a ferny appearance. Eventually, the plant develops ¼-inch-long, bell-like green flowers that are followed by small berries, dark green at first, then maturing to red.

A view of the leaf and fruit of wild asparagus.
JIM ROBERTSON

Uses

Wild and cultivated asparagus are more or less identical. The wild shoots can be used in all the ways in which you'd use store-bought asparagus. They can be steamed or boiled, and served with butter, cheese, or whatever. They can be made into soup or added to soups and stews, and even eaten raw in salads.

The plant is inedible once it has grown to the point of being highly branched.

The red fruits of the mature asparagus plant.
DR. AMADEJ TRNKOCZY

Cautions

Eating raw asparagus shoots and the small red berries causes a mild dermatitis reaction in some individuals. Do not eat the red berries of the maturing plant. Consume only the newly emerging shoots.

CAMAS
Camassia quamash

There are three species of *Camassia* in Idaho, and botanists have defined four subspecies of *C. quamash*. Outside of Idaho, there are several other species of *Camassia*; all are edible. This was formerly classified in the Lily family (Liliaceae), and sometimes classified in the Century Plant family, (Agavaceae).

Use: The bulbs are the traditional food of this plant.
Range: Though once widespread, urban development has wiped out many of the traditional sites. Found in wet and well-drained soils. Common in the grasslands and valleys. Tends to grow in wet soils, rarely in dry soils.
Similarity to toxic species: Death camas; see notes under Cautions.
Best time: Gather the bulbs in late spring to early summer.
Status: Certainly less common than in the past; making a comeback as a garden plant
Tools needed: A trowel or shovel

Properties
Traditionally a part of the Lily family, this perennial lily-like plant consists of a deep bulb from which grass-like leaves arise. The leaves are all basal and flat, up to an inch wide, and anywhere from 5 to 15 inches in length. The flower stalks may be up to 2 feet tall. The purple flowers are over an inch wide, consisting of three sepals and three petals that both look alike, so it appears to have six purple petals. There are six stamens and a three-parted pistil.

As the flower matures, the fruit enlarges, which is a three-lobed dry capsule about an inch long, full of the black seeds.

Though most commonly found in the Columbia Basin, camas grows as far east as Wyoming, and from the British Columbia south into California.

A view of the edible blue camas. JEAN PAWEK

Uses

Camas bulbs—up to an inch in diameter—were once one of the most important foods for the indigenous people of this region. There are still places where you can find them abundantly. When you find them and you want to eat them, dig up the largest and rebury the smaller ones. To be safe, especially if you are just beginning, only dig the bulbs of those plants that are in flower.

You don't eat these raw, or they will cause upset stomach and severe flatulence. They need to be baked for about a day, or more. Traditionally, these were baked from one to three days in a fire pit. A hole is dug, lined with rocks, and a fire is built

Note floral characteristics of the edible blue camas.
ZOYA AKULOVA

and burned for at least three hours. Layers of grass and edible vegetation are laid down, and then a layer of clean cotton can be laid down to keep the bulbs clean. The bulbs are then covered with a layer of more edible vegetation, and covered with soil. You can dig these out in twelve hours or so, but up to three days is better.

John Kallas of Wild Food Adventures found that by cooking the bulbs for nine hours in a pressure cooker at 257 degrees, he produced a sweet tasting bulb. If you don't have a pressure cooker, you can simply try cooking on a stove top, though it takes about 24 hours of cooking to make the bulbs digestible and tasty. The longer the better—just don't let your pan go dry.

The bulbs can be eaten once processed. They can be dried and powdered, and then used in making breads, biscuits, gravy, etc.

In sum, don't eat these raw, and make absolutely certain that you have the right bulb.

Lewis and Clark

The journals have more information about this plant than any other plant the explorers encountered. On September 20, 1805, Clark describes how they were searching for food and came upon an Indian village where they were given buffalo meat, dried berries, and salmon, and some round roots. He described the roots as "much like an onion, which they call quamash the Bread or Cake is called Pas-she-co Sweet, of this they make bread & Supe they also gave us the bread made of this root all of which we eate heartily."

Clark goes on to explain how the camas bulbs were cooked in a traditional fire pit, but doesn't say how long they were cooked. He writes, "I find myself verry unwell all the evening from eateing the fish & roots too freely." Other members of the party also had intestinal pains that lasted for days. The camas roots were probably not cooked long enough.

Once steamed in the pits, Lewis wrote on June 11, 1806, how the camas bulbs were further processed by the Indians. He states that the roots were dried in the sun, where they become black and "of a sweet and agreeable flavor." He adds, "If

A view of the mature camas seed. ROGER GEORGE

the design is to make bread or cakes of the roots they undergo a second process . . . reduced to the consistency of dough and then rolled [into] cakes of eight or ten lbs are returned to the sweat." Once the dough is removed from the fire pit the second time, they are made into little cakes about ½- to ¾-inch thick, and dried in the sun or by the fire. According to Lewis, these cakes "will keep sound for a great length of time. This bread or the dried roots are frequently eaten alone by the natives with further preparation, and when they have them in abundance. they form an ingredient in almost every dish they prepare. This root is palateable but disagrees with me in every shape I have used it."

Cautions

DEATH CAMAS
Zigadenus elegans, Z. venenosus

There is also a plant known as death camas, which closely resembles the edible camas. Death camas typically grows in drier soils, and its flower is greenish-white, often described as yellow. However, the territories of both can overlap.

It's easy to tell these plants apart when they are in flower, but there are reports of indigenous people getting very sick when the death camas bulbs were accidentally dug up and included with the edible bulbs. (Death is apparently somewhat rare if you eat the death camas, but you'll get seriously ill.)

The overall plant—leaves and bulbs—of the death camas is very similar to the edible camas, though the flowers are smaller and greenish-white. In fact, there are at least twenty species of the death camas, mostly in the *Zigadenus* genus, though botanists have been doing a lot of reclassifying of these species.

Bottom line: The edible camas has the blue flower, and can fade to a pale color, somewhat resembling the death camas. If you're uncertain, don't eat it! The death camas will never have the bright blue flower of the edible camas, so if you only collect when the plant is in flower, you'll be okay.

Note the color and floral characteristics of the toxic death camas. JEAN PAWEK

A view of the toxic death camas. JEAN PAWEK

RUSH FAMILY (JUNCACEAE)

The Rush family has seven genera and 440 species worldwide. In Idaho, there are two genera of this family.

RUSH
Juncus textilis, et al.

There are 315 species of *Juncus* worldwide. In Idaho, about fifty-one species (not counting varieties) have been recorded.

Use: Tender white growth at base of shoots edible raw or cooked; seeds cooked in pastry or porridge
Range: Riparian and coastal areas
Similarity to toxic species: In the young stages, there is a superficial resemblance to members of the Lily family, some of which are toxic.
Best time: Spring for the shoots; fall for the seeds
Status: Common locally
Tools needed: A collection bag

A view of the juncus plant while seeding.

Properties

When seeing *Juncus* for the first time, many folks think it's a type of grass or cattail, or they might say "reed." Yes, it has a grass-like appearance, but there are some important differences that put this plant into a different family.

The leaves are long, grass-like, and hollow from top to bottom. There are various lengths of *Juncus*, and *J. textilis* can be found in thick patches up to 5 or 6 feet tall. The leaves are round in the cross-section. The flowers are inconspicuous, bits of seed on the end of long stems, tassel-like, and are formed near the top of each leaf, generally off to one side.

Like many grasses and the cattails, these spread via an underground system of rhizomes. They are typically found in association with wet areas, such as a spring or river, though they are not necessarily right in the water, where you'd find watercress.

Daniela del Valle weaves a cornocopia-style basket from *Juncus* leaves.

Students practice weaving baskets from the rush (*Juncus*) leaves.

Uses

Though this plant and its close relatives are thought of as great weaving and fiber plants, they provide at least two good food sources as well.

In fall, a small tassel of seeds is found on the top portion of the rushes. If you're there at the right time, you can put a bag under the tassel and shake out the seeds. These seeds are then used in the two ways most grains can be used: mixed in with pastry products, or as a cooked cereal.

In spring, when you can gently pull up the long leaves, you will notice that the bottom of the plant is white and tender. There's not a lot of food here, but it's good, and you can get a decent amount in a short period of time. You can eat them raw on the spot, or save them to add to salads, stir-fries, or soups.

Harvesting the shoots seems to make the rush patches grow better, but you still shouldn't just pick these for the tender base and then discard the rest, because you really only get a nibble from each shoot. The upper part of the plant—the long leaves—are great for making traditional baskets. If you're going to eat some of the young bases, you should really collect the shoots and use them for weaving, or give them to someone who makes baskets. Unless, of course, you're lost and starving, which is a whole different situation . . .

FORAGER NOTE: The leaves, properly prepared, are ideal for the traditional basketry done by Native peoples. One of the best "how-to" descriptions of this is found in Paul Campbell's *Survival Skills of Native California.*

LILY FAMILY (LILIACEAE)

AVALANCHE LILY (GLACIER LILY; DOGTOOTH VIOLET)
(Erythronium grandiflorum)

There are about twenty-five recorded species of *Erythronium* genus, found mostly in North America, with at least three species identified in Idaho.

Use: Leaves, flowers, and especially the corms can be eaten.
Range: Widespread. Can be found from Alberta to California. Prefers cool and moist mountain meadows.
Similarity to toxic species: See Cautions.
Best time: Spring
Status: Somewhat common in its environment
Tools needed: Digging tool

Properties
Avalanche lily is sometimes found in dense patches, blooming right after the snowmelt. The plant is perennial, up to a foot tall, with a single pair of opposite leaves near the base. Leaves are about an inch wide and up to 8 inches long. Flowers are yellow to white, with one to four on a single stem. Each flower faces downward. The three sepals and three petals all look alike, so there is the appearance of six yellow petals.

A view of avalanche lilies in the field. H. TIM GLADWIN

Uses

If these are not abundant, it would be best to just leave them alone and enjoy their beauty. Since all of the plant can be eaten, at least do not dig the corms when there are just a few. You can pick some leaves, and even the flowers, and add them to salads or cooked dishes.

Most think of the root as the main food, and these are typically found about a half-foot underground, so a digging tool will be

A view of avalanche lilies in the field.
H. TIM GLADWIN

needed. The flavor is crisp and good, even sweet. You can enjoy them as a nibble, added to salads, or cooked in any way that you'd cook and blend potatoes.

Cautions

The avalanche lily is easy to recognize when it's in flower. However, there are many more bulbs from the Lily family than we have listed here, and some can make you sick, or even kill you. If you dig a bulb from a plant you've not carefully identified, do not assume it is edible. Never eat the bulb of any plant until you have assured yourself that you've positively identified it as an edible bulb, and this can usually only be done when you see the plant in flower.

Lewis and Clark

Of a glacier lily specimen collected by the expedition southeast of Peck, Idaho, Frederick Pursh recorded the following: "From the plains of Columbia near Kooskooskee [today known as Clearwater] R. May 8th 1806. the natives reckon this root as unfitt for food."

A view of the avalanche lily root.
KYLE CHAMBERLAIN

YELLOW BELL
(Fritillaria pudica)

There are about one hundred species of *Fritillaria*. In Idaho, there are three species.

Use: Entire plant is edible; use only if abundant
Range: Open ranges, grassy slopes
Similarity to toxic species: See Cautions
Best time: Spring
Status: Widespread, common
Tools needed: Digging stick

A closeup of the yellowbell flower. JOHN DOYEN

Properties

These are small plants, arising maybe 6 to 8 inches out of the ground from the little bulb. The scaly bulb is usually surrounded by smaller bulbs, each approximately the size of a grain of rice. The narrow linear leaves have parallel veins (as do most monocots), and appear as grass leaves. Sometimes, only two opposite leaves are produced. If there are more leaves, they are alternately arranged.

The growing condition of yellowbells. JOHN DOYEN

Two drooping flowers of the yellowbell. JOHN DOYEN   The yellowbell plant in flower. JOHN DOYEN

Flowers are yellow to orange, aging to a brick red color. The yellow flowers nod downward, and are composed of three sepals and three petals, all identical so the appearance is of a six-petal yellow flower. There are six stamens. The single pistil is divided at the top into a three-part stigma. They are found in dry, open woods, and on slopes.

Uses

The bulb, stalk, leaves, and flower can all be eaten raw or cooked. However, unless really abundant, it's best to just leave these in the ground.

Among the Blackfoot, the bulbs were eaten with soup. Sometimes *F. pudica* was eaten raw, sometimes cooked by steaming or boiling. The fruits can also be dried and stored for later use.

Cautions

Though all *Fritillaria* are generally regarded as edible, among the Ute, a decoction of the bulbs and roots of *F. atropurpurea* is regarded as dangerously poisonous in "large quantities." We were not able to get more data on this, but would appreciate any authenticated reports from readers.

Needless to say, whenever collecting any bulb for food, 100 percent identification is a must since there are many bulbs of different genera that can be poisonous. And positive identification can only be made when the plant is in bloom.

Lewis and Clark

According to Frederick Pursh, specimens of *F. pudica* (yellow bell) were collected on the "Plains of Columbia, near the Kooskooskee [the Clearwater River] on May 8th, 1806." He goes on to say that "the bulb in the Shape of a bisquit, which the natives eat."

MARIPOSA LILY/SEGO LILY
Calochortus spp.

There are about sixty-five species of *Calochortus* in North America. In Idaho, there are ten species, including *C. nuttallii*—the sego lily, also the Utah state flower. The roots of this had been widely used by early Mormons for food.

Use: Bulbs are edible.
Range: Widespread throughout the West
Similarity to toxic species: The plant is distinctive, but if you saw only the bulb, it would be possible to misidentify.
Best time: Spring to summer
Status: Some are rare, some common.
Tools needed: Digging tool

Properties
The small bulb resides deep in the ground, and it seems to prefer harder, rocky ground. Most of the time there's nothing to tell you there are bulbs underneath, except perhaps last year's dried leaves and stalk.

One of the *Calochortus* flowers. LILY JANE TSONG

A view of the *Calochortus* flower. LILY JANE TSONG

In the spring, the grass-like leaves emerge, still somewhat inconspicuous. The leaves are C-shaped in the cross-section. These will rise perhaps a foot tall.

Then the flower emerges, something that tells you, "This is special." It's a beautiful and unique flower, with the typical Lily family pattern of three sepals and three petals. The sepals are pointed and narrower than the petals. The petals can be various colors, from white to pink to orange, and each petal typically has a bit of another color, making the flowers very striking. There are six stamens, and one pistil.

The bulbs are nearly always deeper than you would expect. I'd seen pictures of the mariposa lily before I'd ever seen the real thing, so when I first encountered one, I decided to look at the root. I dug and dug and dug into the hard, rocky hillside, and when I tried to extricate what would have been a tiny bulb, only the stem came out! In such soil, it's better to just leave the bulbs alone and enjoy the floral beauty.

Uses

My recommendation is that you only dig these when they are abundant, and the soil is somewhat loose. Then, you'll need a long digging stick or a narrow spade. Move around as you dig a few in each site. The disturbed soil will actually serve to promote the growth of more bulbs, which Native people learned centuries ago.

Once the bulbs are collected, wash the dirt off and remove the outer skin. They can be eaten raw, or cooked in various dishes. Since they are so small, you'll not usually find enough for a dish of just these, but you can add the cooked bulbs into soups, stews, omelets and other cooked dishes. They are mild-flavored.

Bulbs can also be dried and ground fine into a flour, which you would then use as a thickener for stews, or for any bread or pastry-type items.

GRASS FAMILY (POACEAE)

There are 650 to 900 genera worldwide, with about 10,550 species. A massive group! There are so many species that the family is divided into five or six major categories, depending on the botanist. (Some botanists are joiners, some are splitters, and the splitters seem to be getting the upper hand.) In Idaho, there are over 101 genera, and hundreds of species.

The Grass family has the "greatest economic importance of any family," according to botanist Mary Barkworth, citing wheat, rice, maize, millet, sorghum, sugarcane, forage crops, weeds, and thatching, weaving, and building materials.

Use: Leaves for food (sprouts, juiced, etc.); seeds for flour or meal; some are obviously better than others
Range: Grasses are truly found "everywhere."
Similarity to toxic species: See Cautions.
Best time: Somewhat varies depending on what grass we're talking about, but generally spring for the greens and summer to fall for seed
Status: Very common
Tools needed: A collection bag

A view of one of the many wild grasses found throughout the state.

Mature wild oats.

Properties

The large plant family Poaceae (formerly Gramineae) is characterized by mostly herbaceous but sometimes woody plants with hollow and jointed stems, narrow, sheathing leaves, petal-less flowers borne in spikelets, and fruit in the form of seed-like grain. It includes bamboo, sugarcane, numerous grasses, and cereal grains such as barley, corn, oats, rice, rye, and wheat.

Grasses are generally herbaceous. They can be little annuals to giant bamboos. The stems are generally round and hollow, with swollen nodes. The leaves are alternate, generally narrow, linear, and sheathing. The flowering and seed structures are rather diverse, ranging from the sticky seeds of the foxtail grasses, which get caught in your socks, to the open clusters of sorghum, to such seeds as rice and wheat and the cobs of corn. Indeed, whole books have been written describing the diversity of this large family.

One common example is the common reed, or *Phragmites australis*.

Uses

The edibility of the wild grasses, generically, can be summed up in two categories: the young leaves and the seeds.

You may have had some of the leaf when you went to a health food store and ordered "wheatgrass juice." That's perhaps one of the best ways to eat various grass leaves—juice them. You can purchase an electric juicer or a hand-crank juicer. I have juiced various wild grass leaves and found the flavors to be quite diverse. Some have the flavor of wheatgrass juice, and are good added to drinks or to soup broth. Some are very different, almost like seaweed, and these are typically better in soup.

However you juice it, get the grasses as young as possible. They are most nutritious at this stage, and are less fibrous. You will discover that grasses contain *a lot* of fiber once you start to crank a hand juicer, and watch as the green liquid gold comes out one end and the strands of fiber come out the other end. If you don't have a juicer, you could eat the very young grass leaves in salads or cooked soups, though you may find yourself chewing and chewing and spitting out fiber.

The seeds of all grasses are theoretically edible, though harvesting them is very difficult—if not next to impossible—in some cases. Some grass seeds are easy to collect by hand. They are then winnowed. Some are very easy to winnow of the outer chaff; some are more problematic. I have put "foxtail" grass seeds in a small metal strainer and passed them through a fire in order to burn off the outer covering. Though I was left with a little seed, I found this method less fruitful than simply locating other grasses with more readily harvestable seeds.

In Idaho, you might do best to learn a few common useful grasses at first, like Indian rice grass and fowl manna grass.

Wild rice. ISTOCK.COM

The seeds you gather for food should be mature and have no foreign growths on them. Then you either grind them into flour for pastry products (bread, biscuits, etc.) or cook them into mush, like a cereal mush.

With thousands of species worldwide on every land mass, and large numbers found in Idaho, the grasses are a group that we should get to know better. Not only are they arguably more important than trees in holding the earth together—their combined root systems are vast—but they are a valuable food source, assuming you are there at the right time to harvest the seed or leaf.

Cautions

Be aware that many substances are added to lawns and golf courses to keep the grasses green and bug-free. Those grasses could make you sick, so harvest with caution and common sense. Also, make sure that any seed you harvest is mature, and free of any mold, which will typically give the grain a color such as green, white, or black. Do not eat moldy grass seeds.

Also, note that excessive and prolonged use of certain grasses may have toxic effect: Arrowgrass *Triglocin palustris* contains cyanide compound, prussic acid; Rye grass, *Paspalum dilatatum* may harbor ergot; Fescue from Poaceae may harbor toxic fungus galls; Johnson grass, *Sorghum halepense* contrains prussic acid; and Foxtail *Hordeum jubatum* and other species if now carefully winnowed can pierce and trap in soft tissues. With this in mind, be careful and judicious when foraging.

CATTAIL FAMILY (TYPHACEAE)

The Cattail family contains two genera and about thirty-two species worldwide.

CATTAIL
Typha spp.

The *Typha* genus contains about fifteen species worldwide, with two of those species recorded in Idaho, *T. latifolia* and *T. angustifolia*. *T. domingensis* might also be in Idaho. These all appear very similar.

Use: Food (inner rhizome, young white shoots, green female spike, yellow male pollen); leaves excellent for fiber craft where high tensile strength is not required
Range: Wetlands
Similarity to toxic species: None
Best time: Generally, the shoots and spikes are best collected in the spring. The rhizome could be collected at any time.
Status: Common in wetlands
Tools needed: Clippers; possibly a trowel

David Martinez checks out the mature brown cattail spike.

Properties

Everyone everywhere knows cattail—think of it as that grassy plant in swamps that looks like a hot dog on a stick. Always growing in slow-moving waters or the edges of streams, the plant has long flat leaves that grow up to 6 feet and taller. These long leaves arise from underground horizontal rhizomes. When the plants flower, the flower spike is green, with yellowish pollen at the top. As it matures, the green spike ripens to a brown color, creating the familiar fall decoration: the hot dog on the stick.

Uses

Euell Gibbons used to refer to cattails as the "supermarket of the swamps," which is a good description of this versatile plant. There are at least four good food sources from the cattail, which I'll list in order of my preference.

Green cattail spike. RICK ADAMS

In the spring, the plant sends up its green shoots. If you get to them before they get stiff and before the flower spike has started, you can tug them up and the shoot breaks off from the rhizome. You then cut the lower foot or so and peel off the green layers. The inner white layer is eaten raw or cooked. It looks like a green onion, but the flavor is like cucumber.

The spike is the lower part of the flower spike, technically the female part of the flower. You find the spike in spring, when it's entirely green and tender. Though you could eat it raw, it's far better boiled. Cook it like corn on the cob, butter it, and eat it like corn on the cob. Guess what? It even tastes like corn on the cob. You could also scrape off the green edible portion from the woody core and add to stews or stir-fries, or even shape into patties (with egg or flour added) and cook like burgers.

The pollen is the fine yellow material that you can shake out of the flower spikes. The flower spike is divided into two sections: the lower female part, which can be eaten like corn on the cob, and directly on top, the less-substantial male section, which produces the fine yellow pollen. If you're in the swamp at the right time—typically April or May—you can shake lots of pollen into a bag, strain it (to remove twigs and bugs), and use it in any pastry product.

The rhizome is also a good, starchy food. Get into the mud and pull out the long horizontal roots. Wash them, and then peel off the soft outer layer. You could just chew on the inner part of the rhizome if you need the energy from the

Mature brown cattail spike.

Seeding cattail spikes. In this stage, these spikes are good for stanching wounds, insulation, and tinder.
RICK ADAMS

natural sugar, or you could process it a bit. One method of processing involves mashing or grinding up the inner rhizome, and then putting it into a jar of water. As the water settles, the pure starch will be on the bottom, and the fiber will be floating on top, so you can easily scoop it out and discard it. The starch is then used in soups, or in pastry and bread products.

Aside from cooking, the long green leaves have a long history of being used for various woven products that will not be under tension, such as baskets, sandals, and hats, and even for the outer layers of dwellings utilized by many of the West Coast's Native Americans.

And when that cattail spike matures to a chocolate brown color, it can be broken open and turned into an insulating fluff. Each tiny seed is actually connected to a bit of fluff that aids in the transportation of that seed to

A mature cattail spike.

greener grass on the other side. You can use that fluff to stop the bleeding of a minor wound, as an alternative to down when stuffing a sleeping bag or coat, and as a fantastic fire starter!

SEDGE FAMILY (CYPERACEAE)

The Sedge family contains about one hundred genera, and up to 5,000 species. "Sedges have edges:" Most of the seed stalks are three-sided.

NUT SEDGE
Cyperus esculenta

There are about 600 species of *Cyperus* worldwide. There are eleven recorded species of *Cyperus* in Idaho.

Use: The small underground tubers are edible.
Range: Moist (but not swampy) areas
Similarity to toxic species: None
Best time: Can be collected year-round
Status: Somewhat common
Tools needed: Spade

Nut sedge. LOUIS-M. LANDRY

Properties

Nut grass is a grass-like plant, rising up to 2 feet and found worldwide. The stem is solid and three-sided, as are all sedges. Remember: Sedges have edges. Three to six smaller leaves form a whorl around the base of the flower cluster, which has five to eight rays. The flat, spreading spikelets are straw-colored and numerous. The seeds are ovoid, generally three-angled, and brown. Nut grass grows in wet places, including roadside ditches.

Uses

Sometimes cultivated in other countries, this is generally a pervasive and aggressive weed in croplands and fields. The tubers can be dug, though they are often small. These can be eaten raw, and are more like potatoes when cooked. You can also dry and powder the tubers, and use them as a flour.

Some early wild food references, such as the works of Bradford Angier, seemed to exaggerate both the quality and quantity of this food. It's a viable food, yes, but typically the tubers are very small, and hard to dig. It's best if you can find them in softer or sandier soil, where they are easier to dig and tend to be larger, so you get more for your work.

Sometimes nut grass is cultivated, producing slightly larger tubers. However, you need to love this plant, because once you have it, you'll always have it. In the eyes of many farmers, this plant is a despised nuisance. This is one of the few plants about which I've seen farmers get visibly upset and angry as they talk about it.

OTHER EDIBLES

Do you have a favorite Idaho wild food that wasn't listed here?

Remember, our intent was to include those plants that are the most wide-spread throughout the state and readily recognizable, and those that would make a significant contribution to your day-to-day meals. We also wanted to include plants that represented most of the biological zones in the state. Additionally, we don't want you eating any endangered or rare species, so they've not been included. This book was compiled based on what we ascertained were the plants you are most likely to be eating from the wild, most of the time.

Still, if you feel we've left out an important plant that you have found useful on a regular basis, please write to us and let us know. (See About the Author, p. 266.) If feasible, we'll include that in the next edition of this book.

As you continue your study of ethnobotany, you will discover that there are many more wild plants that could be used for food. Some are marginal, and some just aren't that great.

In fact, there are many other wild Idaho greens, fruits, roots, and nuts that I have eaten, even some that I never found described in a wild food or ethno-botany book. Yes, they are "edible," but after trying them, I realized why ancient people never used them, or only used them when nothing else was available. That's the real meaning of the term *starvation food*—you'd only eat it if you actually had next to nothing else to eat.

Yes, there are many wild animals and ocean life that could be used for food—fish, snakes, lizards, birds, small mammals, insects—but this book is about the plants.

GETTING STARTED

Exploring the Fascinating World of Wild Plants

During the many field trips and classes I have conducted since 1974, I have often been asked how I got interested in the subject of edible wild plants. More importantly, someone will want to know how they should go about learning to identify and use wild foods in the safest and quickest way possible.

Though I had very little prior knowledge of ethnobotany when my interest began (about age twelve or thirteen), I began to seek out local botanists from whom I could learn. I also took every class on this subject, and related subjects, that I could, both in high school and college. In addition, I spent a lot of time in the fields, foothills, mountains, deserts, and on the beaches looking at plants and collecting little samples to take back to my growing body of mentors.

All this took time, and I learned the plants one by one, by the primary method that I still recommend: Show the plant to an expert for identification, or go into the field with an expert so the plant can be identified. Then, once you've identified the plant, you can do all your research in books such as this one, and—assuming it's an edible plant—you can begin to experiment with all the ways to eat it.

I learned some of the very common, widespread plants first, and I would carefully clip samples, take them home, and try them in salad or as cooked greens. Some of the very first plants I began to eat were mustard, miner's lettuce, purslane, and watercress, as these were very common and easy to collect. Once I learned the identity of another edible plant, I would try it in various recipes over the course of the next several weeks, until I felt I "knew" that plant well, and my interests moved on to learning a new plant.

There was no quickie "rule of thumb" for knowing what I could, or could not, eat. There were no lazy-man rules of looking for red in the plant, or the color of the berries, or whether the plant left a bad taste in my mouth. There was simply the effort to discover, to learn one new plant at a time, to utilize that plant in the kitchen, and to watch that plant throughout the growing season so I got to know what it looked like as a sprout, growing up, maturing, flowering, going to seed, and dying. Through observation, I became able to recognize these common floral beings even if I was driving by in a car at a high speed.

So that is what you should do: Seek out a mentor or mentors, study with them, take them plants, get to know the plants, and continue forever with your learning. Use books, videos, and Internet references as a backup to your firsthand interactions with the plants.

Where I grew up, I lived close to the local mountain range, so hiking in the hills was my afterschool or weekend choice of recreation. I began to backpack and carry heavy loads, and found it unpleasant—it's one of those things that you just had to put up with if you wanted to backpack. But then I met a man who talked about how he learned about foods that the Indians of Northern California used in the old days. He mentioned a few specific plants, and something clicked in my brain. I knew that was a skill I had to learn. When I returned from my backpacking trip, I began to research ethnobotany at the local library and museums, and I sought out teachers and mentors.

The fact that I was always interested in the ways of Native Americans, and in practical survival skills, helped immensely. Plus, my mother often told us of the hard times she experienced growing up on the family farm in Ohio. I knew that knowledge of wild foods was an important skill that too many of us had lost.

By January of 1974, I began to lead wild food outings that were organized by WTI, a nonprofit organization focused entirely on education in all aspects of survival. I led half-day walks where we'd go into a small area, identify and collect plants, and make a salad—and maybe soup and tea—on the spot. I became an active member of the local mycological association, and made rapid progress in learning about how to identify and use mushrooms. And I continued to take specialized classes and go on field trips focused on botany, biology, taxonomy, and ethnobotany. I spent many hours in the classroom and lab of Dr. Leonid Enari, who was the chief botanist at the Los Angeles County Arboretum in Arcadia. He was a walking encyclopedia, and he also took the time to mentor me, to answer all my plant questions, and to help me with sections of my first wild food book.

Today, there are many more learning avenues than were available for me, such as the Internet. Most of what I learned, I learned the hard way, in spite of the fact that I had many teachers along the way. So, when I teach, I attempt to provide a way that my students can save time and can learn more rapidly. In short, I try to provide the ideal learning environment that I wished I'd had.

It is to your advantage to completely disregard any of the "rules of thumb" you've ever been taught about plant identification——you know, the shortcuts for determining whether or not a plant is edible. This includes well-intended but incorrect ideas such as: If a plant has a milky sap, it is not edible. If a plant causes an irritation in the mouth when you eat a little, it is not safe to eat. If the animals eat the plants or berries, they are safe to eat. If the berries are white, they are poisonous. If the berries are black or blue, they are safe to eat. And on and on. Disregard all these shortcuts since—although often based on some fact—they all have exceptions. As Spock would say, "Insufficient data." There are no shortcuts to what is necessary: You must study, and you need field experience.

If there is any sort of "shortcut" to the study of plants, it is to learn to recognize plant families, and learn which families are entirely safe for consumption. Beyond that, you must learn plants one by one for absolute safety.

I strongly suggest that you take at least a college course in botany (preferably taxonomy) so you get to know how botanists designate plant families. This will enable you to look at my list of safe families, and then use the books written by botanists who know the flora of your area so you can check to see which plants in that area belong to any of the completely safe families. After a while, this will come easy. Eventually, you'll look at a plant, examine it, and you'll know which family it likely belongs to.

Get a botanical flora book written for your area and study it. In Idaho, there are a few that are used by botanists. See "Useful References" on pages 257–58.

Do your own fieldwork, ideally with someone who already knows the plants. Gradually, eventually, you will use more and more wild plants for food and medicine, and perhaps for soap, fiber, fire, etc. There will be no such thing as a "weed." You will cringe whenever you see television commercials in spring for noxious products, such as Roundup, that promise to kill every dandelion on your property.

When you discover that we have ruined the earth in the name of "modern agriculture," which produces inferior "food," you will understand the meaning of the phrase "We have met the enemy, and he is us."

TEST YOUR KNOWLEDGE OF PLANTS

Here is a simple test that I use in my classes. Take the test for plants and mushrooms and see how you do.

1) ❐ True. ❐ False. Berries that glisten are poisonous.

2) ❐ True. ❐ False. White berries are all poisonous.

3) ❐ True. ❐ False. All blue and black berries are edible.

4) ❐ True. ❐ False. If uncertain about the edibility of berries, watch to see if the animals eat them. If the animals eat the berries, the berries are good for human consumption.

5) Would you follow the following advice? State yes or no, and give your reason.

> According to *Food in the Wilderness* authors George Martin and Robert Scott, "If you do not recognize a food as edible, chew a mouthful and keep it in the mouth. If it is very sharp, bitter, or distasteful, do not swallow it. If it tastes good, swallow only a little of the juice. Wait for about eight hours. If you have suffered no nausea, stomach or intestinal pains, repeat the same experiment swallowing a little more of the juice. Again, wait for eight hours. If there are no harmful results, it probably is safe for you to eat. (This test does not apply to mushrooms.)"

6) ❐ True. ❐ False. "A great number of wilderness plants are edible but generally they have very little food value." [Martin and Scott, ibid.]

7) ❐ True. ❐ False. Bitter plants are poisonous.

8) ❐ True. ❐ False. Plants that exude a milky sap when cut are all poisonous.

9) ❐ True. ❐ False. Plants that cause stinging or irritation on the skin are all unsafe for consumption.

10) The illustration to the right is the typical flower formation for all members of the Mustard family. Write out the formula:

_____ petal(s); _____ sepal(s);

_____ stamen(s); _____ pistil(s).

PISTIL   STAMENS

← PETALS

← SEPALS

11) Of what value is it to be able to identify the Mustard family?

12) ❑ True. ❑ False. Mustard (used on hot dogs) is made by grinding up the yellow flowers of the mustard plant.

13) ❑ True. ❑ False. Yucca, century plant, and prickly pear are all members of the Cactus family.

14) ❑ True. ❑ False. There are no poisonous cacti.

15) ❑ True. ❑ False. Plants that resemble parsley, carrots, and fennel are all in the Carrot (or Parsley) family and are thus all safe to eat.

16 ❑ True. ❑ False. Only seventeen species of acorns are edible. The rest are toxic.

17) To consume acorns, the tannic acid must first be removed. Why?

18) If you are eating no meat or dairy products (during a survival situation, for example), how is it possible to get complete protein from plants alone?

19) ❑ True. ❑ False. There are no toxic grasses.

20) ❑ True. ❑ False. Seaweeds are unsafe survival foods.

21) ❑ True. ❑ False. All plants that have the appearance of a green onion and have the typical onion aroma can be safely eaten.

22) List all of the plant families (or groups) from this lesson that we've identified as entirely or primarily nontoxic:

ANSWERS

1. False. Insufficient data.

2. False. Though mostly true, there are exceptions such as white strawberry, white mulberry, and others. Don't eat any berry unless you know its identity and you know it to be edible.

3. False. Mostly true, but there are some exceptions. Don't eat any berry unless you've identified it as an edible berry.

4. False, for several reasons. Certain animals are able to consume plants that would cause sickness or death in a human. Also, animals do occasionally die from eating poisonous plants—especially during times of drought. Also, just because you watched the animal eat a plant doesn't mean the animal didn't get sick later!

5. Very bad advice, even though this has been repeated endlessly in "survival manuals" and magazine articles. Because food is rarely your top "survival priority," this is potentially dangerous advice.

6. False. To verify that this is untrue, look at *Composition of Foods*, which is published by the US Department of Agriculture. In many cases, wild foods are far more nutritious than common domesticated foods.

7. False. Insufficient data. Many bitter plants are rendered edible and palatable simply by cooking or boiling.

8. False. Though you can't eat any of the *Euphorbia* genus, many other plants (like dandelion, lettuce, milkweed, sow thistle) exude a milky sap. Forget about such "shortcuts." Get to know the individual plants.

9. False. Many edible plants have stickers or thorns that must first be removed, or cooked away, such as nettles and cacti.

10. Mustard flowers are composed of 4 sepals (one under each petal); 4 petals (the colorful part of the flower); 1 pistil (in the very center of flower, the female part of the flower); and 6 stamens (which surround the pistil), 4 are tall, and 2 are short.

11. There are no poisonous members of the Mustard family.

12. False. The mustard condiment is made by grinding the seeds. Yellow is typically from food coloring.

13. False. Only the prickly pear is a cactus.

14. True, but you must know what is, and is not, a cactus. There are some very bitter narcotic cacti that you would not eat due to unpalatability. Also, some *Euphorbia* closely resemble cacti and will cause sickness if eaten. *Euphorbia*

exude a milky sap when cut; cacti do not. Any fleshy, palatable part of true cacti can be eaten.

15. False. The Carrot family contains both good foods and deadly poisons. Never eat any wild plant resembling parsley unless you have identified that specific plant as an edible species.

16. False. All acorns can be consumed once the tannic acid is removed.

17 Tannic acid is bitter.

18. Combine the seeds from grasses with the seeds from legumes. This generally produces a complete protein. For more details, see *Diet for a Small Planet* by Frances Moore Lappé.

Traditional Diets That Combine Legumes and Grass Seeds to Make a Complete Protein

Loosely based upon "Summary of Complementary Protein Relationships," Chart X in *Diet for a Small Planet* by Lappé

	Legumes	Grasses
Asian diet	Soy (miso, tofu, etc.)	Rice
Mexican diet	Beans (black beans, etc.)	Corn (tortillas)
Middle East diet	Garbanzos	Wheat
Southern United States	Black eyed peas	Grits
Starving student	Peanut butter	Wheat bread
Others to consider	Mesquite, palo verde, peas, carob, etc.	Millet, rye, oats, various wild grasses, etc.

19. True, however, be certain that the seeds are mature and have no mold-like growth on them.

20. False. Seaweeds are excellent. Make certain they've not been rotting on the beach, and don't collect near any sewage treatment facilities.

21. True. But be sure you have an onion!

22. All members of the Mustard family, all palatable cacti, all acorns, all cattails, grasses, seaweeds, onions. There are many other "safe" families, but you will need to do a bit of botanical study to identify those families. Begin by reading the descriptions of each family in this book. Also consider reading *Botany in a Day: The Patterns Method of Plant Identification* by Tom Elpel.

THE EASIEST-TO-RECOGNIZE, MOST WIDESPREAD, MOST VERSATILE WILD FOODS OF IDAHO

In the mid-1970s, I began to investigate the edibility of whole plant families, and found that there were quite a few entire families that are safe to eat, given a few considerations in each case. Some of these families are difficult to recognize unless you are a trained botanist. Still, in this book I have described many of the entirely safe families. My original research on this was done with Dr. Leonid Enari, who was one of my teachers and the chief botanist at the Los Angeles County Arboretum in Arcadia, California.

The chart on pp. 249-50 was the idea of my friend Jay Watkins, who long urged me to produce a simple handout on the most common edible plants that everyone should know. Granted, there are many more than a dozen, but as Jay and I discussed this idea, I decided to focus on the plants that could be found not just anywhere in the United States, but in most locales throughout the world. The result was the accompanying chart, which is largely self-explanatory.

This chart assumes that you already know these plants, since its purpose is not identification. Anyone who has studied wild foods for a few years is probably already familiar with all these plants. However, not everyone is aware that these plants are found worldwide.

This overview should help beginners as well as specialists. It is merely a simple comparative chart, which could be expanded to many, many pages. It is deliberately kept short and simple.

	Description	Parts used	Food uses	Preparation	Benefits	Where found	When found
Cactus	Succulent desert plants of various shapes	Tender parts; fruit	Salad; cooked vegetable; omelet; dessert; drinks	1. Carefully remove spines 2. Dice or slice as needed	Pads said to be good for diabetics; fruits rich in sugar	Dry desert-like environments; Mediterranean zones	Young green pads in spring and summer; fruit in summer and fall
Cattail	Reed-like plants; fruit looks like hot dog on stick	1. Pollen 2. Green flower spike 3. Tender shoots 4. Rhizome	1. Flour 2. Cooked vegetable 3. Salads 4. Flour	1. Shake out pollen 2. Boil 3. Remove outer green fibrous parts 4. Remove outer parts and crush	Widespread and versatile	Wet areas, e.g., roadside ditches, marshes	Spring through fall
Chickweed	Weak-stemmed, opposite leaves, five-petaled flower	Entire tender plant	Salads, tea	Clip, rinse, and add dressing, or make infusion	Good diuretic	Common and widespread when moisture is present	Spring and summer
Dandelion	Low plant, toothed leaves, conspicuous yellow flower	1. Roots 2. Leaves	1. Cooked vegetable, coffee-like beverage 2. Salads, cooked vegetable	1. Clean and cook; or dry, roast, grind 2. Clean and make desired dish	Richest source of beta carotene; very high in vitamin A	Common in lawns and fields	Best harvested in spring
Dock	Long leaves with wavy margins	1. Leaves 2. Stems 3. Seeds	1. Salads, cooked vegetable 2. Pie 3. Flour	1. Clean 2. Use like rhubarb 3. Winnow seeds	Richer in vitamin C than oranges	Common in fields and near water	Spring through fall
Grasses	Many widespread varieties	1. Seeds 2. Leaves	1. Flour, mush 2. Salads, juiced, cooked vegetable	1. Harvest and winnow 2. Harvest, clean, and chop	1. Easy to store 2. Rich in many nutrients	Common in all environments	1. Fall 2. Spring

	Description	Parts used	Food uses	Preparation	Benefits	Where found	When found
Lamb's-quarter	Triangular leaves with toothed margins, mealy surface	1. Leaves and tender stems 2. Seeds	1. Salads, soups, omelets, cooked 2. Bread, mush	1. Harvest and clean 2. Winnow	Rich in vitamin A and calcium	Likes disturbed rich soils	Spring through fall
Mustard	Variable leaves with large terminal lobes; four-petaled flowers	Leaves, seeds, some roots	Salads, cooked dishes, seasoning	Gather, clean, cut as needed	Said to help prevent cancer	Common in fields and many environments	Spring through fall
Onions	Grass-like appearance; flowers with three petals, three sepals	Leaves, bulbs	Seasoning, salads, soups, vegetable dishes	Clean and remove tough outer leaves	Good for reducing high blood pressure and high cholesterol levels	Some varieties found in all environments	Spring
Purslane	Low-growing succulent, paddle-shaped leaves	All tender portions	Salads, sautéed, pickled, soups, vegetable dishes	Rinse off any soil	Richest source of omega-3 fatty acids	Common in parks, gardens, disturbed soils	Summer

Latin Names: Cattail = *Typha* spp.; Chickweed = *Stellaria media*; Dandelion = *Taraxacum officinale*; Dock = *Rumex crispus*; Grasses = Poaceae (Grass family); Lamb's-quarter = *Chenopodium album*; Mustard = *Brassica* spp. / Mustard family = Cruciferae; Onions = *Allium* spp.; Purslane = *Portulaca oleracea*

STAFF OF LIFE:
BEST WILD-FOOD BREAD SOURCES

The baking of bread goes back to the most ancient cultures on the earth, back when humankind discovered that you could grind up the seeds of grasses, add a few other ingredients, let the dough rise, and bake it. There are countless variations, of course, but bread was once so nutritious that it became known as the "staff of life."

Most likely, the discovery of bread predated agriculture, since the earth was full of wild grasses and a broad assortment of roots and seeds that could be baked into nutritious loafs. Most grains store well for a long time, which allowed people the time to pursue culture, inner growth, and technology. The development of civilizations and the development of agriculture go hand in hand. And bread was right there from the beginning.

Today, we are at another extreme of a very long road of human development. We started with the struggle for survival, and the surplus of the land allowed us the time to develop more fully in all aspects. That good bread from the earth was heavy, rich, extremely nutritious. It was a vitamin and mineral tablet.

We produced so much grain that the United States began to call itself "the breadbasket of the world." This massive volume suffered losses in the fields from insects due to spoilage. Thus came the so-called Green Revolution, where chemical fertilizers replaced time-honored fertilizers such as animal manures, straw and hay, compost, bone meal, and other such natural substances that the farmer became too busy and too modern to use. Crops increased while the nutritional values dropped. Though this is a gross oversimplification, bread from the supermarket is no longer the staff of life.

The mineral content of the once-rich soils of the United States has steadily declined. Producers process and refine "white flour," and then add certain minerals back in to the bread dough. We sacrificed quality since we thought it would bring us security, and we knew it would bring big bucks. Now, the great irony is that we lost the quality of the food, of the soil, and ultimately we are no more secure than ever before. Why? Because a soil rich in natural organic matter can withstand floods and droughts and the ravages of insects. It is the folly of man who causes the droughts and plagues of modern times.

There is much—very much—that we need to learn about "modern agriculture," or "agribiz" as it is more appropriately called. We should not put our heads into the sand, ostrich-like, and pretend the problem does not exist.

Personal solutions are many. Grow your own garden. Learn about wild foods, and use them daily. By using common wild plants, you can create a nutritious bread comparable to the breads your ancestors ate. The easiest way to get started is to make flour from wild seeds and mix that flour half-and-half with conventional flours, such as wheat. You'll end up with a more flavorful, more nutritious bread, pancake, or pastry product.

Once you begin to use local wild grains, you'll be amazed how tasty, how abundant, and how versatile these wild foods are.

The accompanying chart is by no means complete. It is a general guideline to show you what is available over widespread areas. However, there are quite a few plants of limited range that produce abundant seeds or other parts that are suitable in bread-making. In most cases, you should consult any of the many wild food cookbooks available for details on using each of these wild grains.

Note that "Grass" is a huge category, since it actually includes many of our domestic grains such as wheat, corn, rye, barley, etc. Though some of the seeds listed in this chart can be eaten raw, most require some processing before you can eat them. The seed from amaranth, dock, and lamb's-quarter can get somewhat bitter and astringent as it gets older, and is improved by cooking.

By rediscovering the wealth of wild plants that are found throughout this country, we can bring bread back to its status as the "staff of life."

RECIPE

Beginner Wild Bread Recipe

1 cup whole wheat flour

1 cup wild flour of your choice

3 teaspoons baking powder

3 tablespoons honey

1 egg

1 cup milk

3 tablespoons oil

Salt to taste, if desired

Mix all the ingredients well and bake in oiled bread pans for about 45 minutes at 250°F or in your solar oven until done.

Beginner Pancake Recipe

Follow the above recipe, adding extra milk or water so you have pancake batter consistency. Make pancakes as normal.

"Wild Bread" Chart

	Part Used	How Processed	Where Found	Palatability	Ability to Store
Acorns	Shelled acorns	Leach acorns of tannic acid by soaking or boiling, and grind into meal	Worldwide; ripens in fall	Good, if fully leached	Excellent
Amaranth	Seeds	Collect and winnow seeds	Worldwide as a weed of disturbed soils	Good	Very good
Cattail	Pollen and rhizome	Shake the top of cattail spikes into bag to collect pollen; mash peeled rhizome and separate out fiber	Worldwide in wet and marshy areas	Very good	Good
Dock	Seeds	Collect brown seeds in fall, rub to remove "wings," and winnow	Worldwide in wet areas and disturbed soils	Acceptable	Very good
Grass—most species	Seeds	Generally, simply collect and winnow; difficulty depends on species	Worldwide; some found in nearly every environment	Generally very good	Very good to excellent
Lamb's-quarter	Seeds	Collect when leaves on plant are dry; rub between hands and winnow	Worldwide in disturbed soils and farm soils	Acceptable to good	Very good

Note: This chart is intended only as a general guideline to compare sources for "wild bread" ingredients. There may be many other wild plants that can be used for bread. Also, never eat any wild plant that you have not positively identified as an edible species.

Latin names: Acorns = *Quercus* spp.; Amaranth = *Amaranthus* spp.; Cactus = primarily *Opuntia* spp. and other Cactaceae; Cattail = *Typha* spp.; Dock = *Rumex crispus*; Grass = Poaceae; Lamb's-quarter = *Chenopodium album*.

SWEET TOOTH: BEST WILD-FOOD SUGARS AND DESSERTS

When people speak of "sugar" today, they are almost always talking about the highly refined, nutrition-free white substance made from sugarcane or sugar beets. Unfortunately, modern sugar is a foodless-food. It is the "cocaine" of the modern human's dinner plate. It is not good for the body, and it offers no nutrients whatsoever. But this has not always been so.

Just a few generations ago, it was common for people to make their own sugars. Every culture had their favorite sources for their sugars, depending on what was found in the wild or what was grown in that particular location. In most cases, they simply collected, dried, and ground up sugar-rich fruits. Most such fruits will naturally crystallize with time, and then could be further ground. The advantage of these sugars over "white cane sugar" is that these sugars had their own individual flavors, and they contained many valuable minerals.

Some sugars are quite simple to "produce," such as honey. The main obstacles are finding a way to house the bees—something modern beekeepers do quite well—and finding a way to keep from getting stung. Tapping maple trees (and several other trees) was so simple that even the North American Native peoples did it. They simply cut narrow slashes into the tree, inserted hollow tubes made from elder branches, and collected the sap in whatever containers they had. Raw maple sap is usually boiled down to a syrup of desired consistency and sugar content. Sometimes you may boil off about 40 gallons of water for each gallon of syrup. You do *not* do this indoors.

People have always sought ways to make foods more flavorful, and sugar is certainly useful in that regard. But sugar is also valuable as a preservative. Both sugar and salt help to preserve foods and keep them from spoiling. This was especially important in the past when there was no electricity or refrigerators.

It's amazing how fast a modern culture forgets things. Probably not one in a thousand urbanites knows these simple details about sugar. Our culture has sunk to such ignorance in this matter that we somehow believe that the only choice is between the pink or blue packet. Rather than produce nutritious sugars as we have in the past, the trend is to produce high-tech sweet substances that not only have no nutrients but have no calories either, as does white sugar. The wonders of science never cease!

For those of you who want to try making sugar, the accompanying chart (p. 256) gives you some ideas as to what is available. Currants and gooseberries were very popular among Native Americans not as a sweetener but as a preservative. They ground up jerky and added ground-up currants or gooseberries, and the result was pemmican.

Though many of the wild berries described in the chart have been used as sweeteners for other foods, most of them are good foods in their own right, and have long been used to make such things as drinks, pies, jams, custards, and a variety of dessert items. Details for uses can be found in many of the wild food cookbooks available.

Here's one recipe, which can be used with all of the sugars in the chart, with the exception of manzanita. Manzanita does not produce fleshy berries, so they won't cook up like the others.

RECIPE

Northwest Brickle

½ gallon ripe blackberries

Water to cover berries

½ cup honey

Approximately ⅓ cup biscuit mix

Begin by gently cooking the washed berries. When they are cooked, add the honey and stir. After the mixture thickens, stir in the biscuit mix little by little. The mix will be very thick when it is ready to serve.

This makes a heavy, sweet dessert. In the old days, what wasn't eaten would be put into a bread pan and baked until dry so it would store. It would then last a long time until reconstituted. The dried shape looked like a brick, which is the source of the name.

"Wild Sugar" Chart

	Part Used	How Processed	Where Found	Sweetness / Palatability	Ability to Store
Apples, Wild (including crab apples)	Whole fruit	Use fresh, or slice, dry, and grind to flour	Entire US	Very good; collect when ripe	Very good
Berries (blackberries, raspberries, thimbleberries)	Whole fruit	Use fresh, or dry and grind	Entire US	Excellent	Very good
Currants	Whole fruit	Use fresh, or dry and store	Entire US	Good	Very good
Elder	Whole fruit	Can use fresh if cooked first, or dry and store	Entire US	Contains sugar but tart	Good
Gooseberries	Whole fruit	Remove spiny layer, then use fresh, or dry	Entire US	Good	Very good
Grapes, Wild	Whole fruit	Use fresh, or dry	Most of the US	Sometimes tart; collect ripe fruit	Very good
Maple	Sap	Cut bark on tree and capture sap; use fresh; crystallizes naturally	Entire US, but best flow where there is snow	Excellent	Excellent
Prickly Pear Cactus	Fruit	Remove stickers, use inner pulp fresh or dried, with or without seed	Entire US, but most common in Southwest	Excellent	Good

Note: Many sugars are found in nature, usually in the fruits. Honey is a traditional sugar made indirectly from plant nectars. Other traditional sugars include dried and powdered dates, dried pomegranate juice, and beets. This chart compares a few wild sugar sources that are the most widespread throughout North America. There are many plants that are either marginal sugar sources or available in very limited locations. Never use any wild plant for sugar or food until you have positively identified it as an edible plant.

Latin names: Apples, wild = *Malus* spp.; Berries = *Rubus* spp.; Elder = *Sambucus* spp.; Gooseberries = *Ribes* spp.; Grapes, wild = *Vitis* spp.; Maple = *Acer* spp.; Prickly pear cactus = *Opuntia* spp.

USEFUL REFERENCES

Angier, Bradford. *Free for the Eating.* Mechanicsburg, PA: Stackpole Books, 1996.

Baldwin, Bruce G., et al., eds. *The Jepson Manual, Vascular Plants of California.* 2nd ed. Berkeley: University of California Press, 2012. This is the book botanists of California use, and a vast majority of the plants in Idaho can also be found in California.

Benoliel, Doug. *Northwest Foraging: The Classic Guide to Edible Plants of the Northwest.* Seattle: Skipstone Books, 2011. Benoliel covers more than fifty plants in this guide to Northwest edibles, which includes line drawings and a section on poisonous plants. No marginal foods included.

Deur, Douglas. *Pacific Northwest Foraging: 120 Wild and Flavorful Edibles from Alaska Blueberries to Wild Hazelnuts.* Timber Press. 2014. Beautiful photographs and full of useful information and personal experience.

Elpel, Tom. *Botany in a Day: The Patterns Method of Plant Identification.* Pony, Montana: HOPS Press, 2000. Highly recommended: This is the way botany should be taught.

Elpel, Tom, and Kris Reed. *Foraging the Mountain West.* Pony, Montana: HOPS Press, 2014. A lively exploration of the wild foods of the Northwest.

Enari, Dr. Leonid. *Plants of the Pacific Northwest.* Portland, Oregon: Binfords and Mort, 1956. Written by Dr. Enari after he moved to Portland from Estonia, this book covers 663 weeds, wildflowers, shrubs, and trees that are common in the Northwest. Includes 185 line drawings, which means that most plants are not illustrated.

Garcia, Cecilia, and James D. Adams Jr. *Healing with Medicinal Plants of the West: Cultural and Scientific Basis for Their Use.* La Crescenta, California: Abedus Press, 2005. An excellent summary of the common edible and medicinal plant uses found in the west.

Hitchcock, C. Leo, and Arthur Cronquist. *Flora of the Pacific Northwest.* Seattle: University of Washington Press, 1981. This is the book the botanists of Oregon, Washington, and Idaho use. As a book of flora goes, it's designed as a key so you can (hopefully) identify the plant you've found. Mostly botanical text and technical line drawings throughout. Also has a good glossary (you'll need it).

Kallas, John. *Edible Wild Plants: Wild Foods from Dirt to Plate.* Salt Lake City: Gibbs Smith, 2010. Though this book covers only fifteen wild foods, they are some of the most common wild foods not only in Idaho but throughout the United States. The full-color book tells you everything from identifying the plant to using it in a variety of recipes. Kallas also teaches classes and is the go-to guy for the Pacific Northwest when it comes to wild foods! Reach John Kallas, director of Wild Food Adventures at Institute for the Study of Edible Wild Plants and Other Foragables, 422 SE 49th Ave, Portland, OR 97215; (503) 775-3828; www.wildfoodadventures.com.

Kirk, Donald. *Wild Edible Plants of Western North America.* Happy Camp, California: Naturegraph, 1970. Though you generally cannot positively identify plants with this book, it does contain a large number of edible and useful plant descriptions, along with drawings that leave a lot to the imagination. Get this book, and use another book to positively identify the plants.

Moerman, Daniel E. *Native American Ethnobotany.* Portland, Oregon: Timber Press, 1998. Nearly a thousand pages of descriptions of how every plant known to be used by Native Americans was utilized. No pictures at all, but an incredible resource all in one book.

Nyerges, Christopher. *Foraging Wild Edible Plants of North America*, A Falcon Guide, 2016

———. *Foraging Washington*, A Falcon Guide. 2017

———. *Guide to Wild Foods and Useful Plants*, Chicago Review Press, 2014

H. Phillips Wayne. *Plants of the Lewis and Clark Expedition.* Mount Press Publishing Co., 2003. An excellent botanical journey along the Lewis and Clark expedition of 1804-1806.

Taylor, Ronald J. *Northwest Weeds: The Ugly and Beautiful Villains of Fields, Gardens, and Roadsides.* Missoula, Montana: Mountain Press Publishing, 1990. An excellent full-color summary of some of the common plants of the Northwest, organized by families.

Vascular Plants of Idaho. A checklist of what grows in Idaho, with maps of reported sightings, and photos. www.pnwherbaria.org/m/datasets/vascular plants/lists/id.htm.

Washington Flora Checklist: A Checklist of the Vascular Plants of Washington State. Hosted by the University of Washington Herbarium. http://biology.burke.washington.edu/herbarium/waflora/checklist.php.

INDEX

ABOUT THE AUTHOR

Christopher Nyerges, co-founder of the School of Self-Reliance, has led wild food and survival skills walks for thousands of students since 1974. He has authored sixteen books, mostly on wild foods, survival, and self-reliance, and thousands of newspaper and magazine articles. He continues to teach where he lives in Los Angeles County, California. More information about classes and seminars is available at www.SchoolofSelf-Reliance.com, or by writing to School of Self-Reliance, Box 41834, Eagle Rock, CA 90041.